29 Leadership Secrets from Jack Welch

Abridged from
Get Better or Get Beaten,
SECOND EDITION

Robert Slater

McGraw-Hill

New York   Chicago   San Francisco   Lisbon   London   Madrid
Mexico City   Milan   New Delhi   San Juan   Seoul
Singapore   Sydney   Toronto

The **McGraw·Hill** *Companies*

Library of Congress Cataloging-in-Publication Data

Library of Congress Cataloging-in-Publication Data has been applied for.

    4 5 6 7 8 9 0   AGM/AGM   0 9 8 7 6 5 4 3

ISBN 0-07-140937-8

McGraw-Hill books are available at special discounts to use as premiums and sales promotions, or for use in corporate training programs. For more information, please write to the Director of Special Sales, Professional Publishing, McGraw-Hill, Two Penn Plaza, New York, NY 10121-2298. Or contact your local bookstore.

 This book is printed on recycled, acid-free paper containing a minimum of 50% recycled de-inked paper.

CONTENTS

Preface   vii

PART I

THE VISIONARY LEADER: MANAGEMENT TACTICS FOR GAINING THE COMPETITIVE EDGE

LEADERSHIP SECRET **1** Harness the Power of Change   3

LEADERSHIP SECRET **2** Face Reality!   8

LEADERSHIP SECRET **3** Managing Less Is Managing
                         Better   12

LEADERSHIP SECRET **4** Create a Vision and Then Get
                         Out of the Way   15

LEADERSHIP SECRET **5** Don't Pursue a Central Idea;
                         Instead, Set Only a Few Clear,
                         General Goals as Business
                         Strategies   19

LEADERSHIP SECRET **6** Nurture Employees Who
                         Share the Company's Values   23

PART II

IGNITING A REVOLUTION: STRATEGIES FOR DEALING WITH CHANGE

LEADERSHIP SECRET **7** Keep Watch for Ways to Create
                         Opportunities and to Become
                         More Competitive   29

LEADERSHIP SECRET **8** Be Number One or Number
                         Two and Keep Redefining Your
                         Market   33

LEADERSHIP SECRET **9** Downsize, Before It's Too Late! 37

LEADERSHIP SECRET **10** Use Acquisitions to Make the
Quantum Leap! 41

LEADERSHIP SECRET **11** Learning Culture I: Use
Boundarylessness and
Empowerment to Nurture a
Learning Culture 46

LEADERSHIP SECRET **12** Learning Culture II: Inculcate the
Best Ideas into the Business, No
Matter Where They Come From 50

LEADERSHIP SECRET **13** The Big Winners in the
Twenty-first Century Will
Be Global 54

PART III

REMOVING THE BOSS ELEMENT: PRODUCTIVITY SECRETS FOR CREATING THE BOUNDARYLESS ORGANIZATION

LEADERSHIP SECRET **14** De-Layer: Get Rid of the Fat! 61

LEADERSHIP SECRET **15** Spark Productivity Through the
"S" Secrets (Speed, Simplicity,
and Self-Confidence) 65

LEADERSHIP SECRET **16** Act Like a Small Company 69

LEADERSHIP SECRET **17** Remove the Boundaries! 73

LEADERSHIP SECRET **18** Unleash the Energy of Your
Workers 77

LEADERSHIP SECRET **19** Listen to the People Who
Actually Do the Work 81

LEADERSHIP SECRET **20** Go Before Your Workers and
Answer All Their Questions 86

PART IV

NEXT GENERATION LEADERSHIP: INITIATIVES FOR DRIVING AND SUSTAINING DOUBLE-DIGIT GROWTH

LEADERSHIP SECRET **21** Stretch: Exceed Your Goals as Often as You Can — 93

LEADERSHIP SECRET **22** Make Quality a Top Priority — 97

LEADERSHIP SECRET **23** Make Quality the Job of Every Employee — 101

LEADERSHIP SECRET **24** Make Sure Everyone Understands How Six Sigma Works — 105

LEADERSHIP SECRET **25** Make Sure the Customer Feels Quality — 110

LEADERSHIP SECRET **26** Grow Your Service Business: It's the Wave of the Future — 115

LEADERSHIP SECRET **27** Take Advantage of E-Business Opportunities — 119

LEADERSHIP SECRET **28** Make Existing Businesses Internet-Ready—Don't Assume That New Business Models Are the Answer — 123

LEADERSHIP SECRET **29** Use E-Business to Put the Final Nail in Bureaucracy — 127

Afterword — 133

PREFACE

Jack Welch, the long-time Chairman and CEO of General Electric, has been hailed as the greatest business leader of our era and deservedly so. It was Welch who headed GE from April 1981 to September 2001 and who pioneered some of the most important business strategies of the past two decades. We now take these strategies for granted as part of the way American business is done: restructuring, the emphasis on being number one or number two, making quality a top priority (through his Six Sigma initiative), and so on. Moreover, Welch, unlike most other business leaders, created a tightly woven, carefully scripted business philosophy that provided brief, crisp guidelines for every aspect of business.

Welch's main leadership secrets, spelled out in this book, continue to resonate throughout the business world. Few other business leaders have articulated how to achieve maximum performance with such clarity and forthrightness.

Before Welch took over at GE, the business world had revered large bureaucracies as critical for close monitoring of personnel; it had placed great faith in a command-and-control management system, encouraging senior management to overmanage; it had allowed the employee to attain a protected status by being assured of a job for life. Jack Welch punctured holes in each of these notions. His legacy is that he has forever altered these myths and has inspired managers of corporations around the world to behave far differently: Bureaucracies are much smaller, with fewer management layers; managers manage much less, delegating far greater authority to empowered employees; the right to a job for life is no longer guaranteed as management runs much tighter, more productive ships.

Welch's performance at General Electric lent mighty credence to his ideas: When he assumed the post of Chairman and CEO of GE, the company had annual sales of $25 billion and earnings of $1.5 billion, with a $12 billion market value, tenth best among

American public companies. In 2000, the year before Welch retired, GE had $129.9 billion in revenues; and $12.7 billion in earnings. In 2001, GE's revenues stood at $125.9 billion; and earnings rose to $14.1 billion.

From 1993 until the summer of 1998, GE was America's market cap leader. Under Welch, the company reached a high of $598 billion in market cap (but settled in at about $400 billion during Welch's final years as CEO). *Fortune* magazine selected GE as "America's Greatest Wealth Creator" from 1998 to 2000.

Anyone in business, from the most powerful corporate managers to the hourly factory worker, has much to learn from Jack Welch and his ideas. Studying his leadership secrets tells us what American business was once like, and outlines how the tactics he pioneered have changed business for the better in so many ways.

PART I

THE VISIONARY LEADER:
MANAGEMENT TACTICS FOR GAINING
THE COMPETITIVE EDGE

LEADERSHIP SECRET 1

HARNESS THE POWER OF CHANGE

FROM THE FILES OF JACK WELCH

The mindset of yesterday's manager—accepting compromise, keeping things tidy—bred complacency. Tomorrow's leaders must raise issues, debate them, and resolve them. They must rally around a vision of what a business can become.

Is there a secret formula for succeeding in business? Probably not. But it makes sense to study a master—the man widely regarded as the ablest business leader of the modern era. And that person is Jack Welch, the recently retired CEO and chairman of General Electric.

"Perhaps the most admired CEO of his generation," *Fortune* magazine said of Welch in its May 1, 2000, edition.

How did Welch earn this kind of praise?

BRINGING IN BIG NUMBERS

When he took over at General Electric in 1981, the company had sales of "only" $25 billion. In 1999, GE's sales reached nearly $112 billion. Its profits in 1981 were $1.5 billion; Welch grew the bottom line to nearly $11 billion in 1999.

Welch wasn't just "doing something right." To hit those kinds of numbers, he did *many* things right. He had great ideas, and he implemented them.

In the balance of this book, we spell out those ideas in detail. Yes, Welch led a huge enterprise with 340,000 employees, but we believe that his ideas can be put to work in organizations of all sizes.

Of all of Jack Welch's ideas, none carries more weight than this: *Change, before it's too late!*

Change is easy, right? The boss makes a decision, and employees implement it—right?

If you're in business, you know that change almost never works like that. In fact, it can be the most difficult thing in the world. Welch understood this fact, and yet he pushed for change almost from the minute he took over at GE in the spring of 1981.

CHANGE WAS EVERYWHERE

Change was rampant in the early 1980s. Inflation was raging, and global competitors were capturing unprecedented market shares.

Welch understood the challenges his company faced:

> **It was a reminder that we'd better get a lot better, faster.**
> **So I guess my message in our company was, "The game is going to change, and change drastically." And we had to get a plan, a program together, to deal with a decade that was totally different.**

What did this mean for GE?

New products, a different business environment every day, and a company within which *every employee had to embrace change.*

MAKE EACH DAY YOUR FIRST DAY ON THE JOB

Welch loved to tell GE executives to start their day as if it were their first day on the job.

In other words, always think fresh thoughts. Make it a habit to think about your business. Don't rest on your laurels.

Make whatever changes are necessary to improve things. Re-examine your agenda, and rewrite what needs to be rewritten.

To many both inside and outside the company, it appeared that Welch could have left well enough alone. After all, GE was a model corporation, right?

Welch knew better:

> **I could see a lot of [GE] businesses becoming . . . lethargic. American business was inwardly focused on the bureaucracy.**
>
> **[That bureaucracy] was right for its time, but the times were changing rapidly. Change was occurring at a much faster pace than business was reacting to it.**

THE GENESIS OF "NUMBER ONE, NUMBER TWO"

Welch responded by coming up with a new strategy for GE's businesses. From then on, he announced, those businesses would have to be either number one or number two in their market. If they couldn't hit that high standard, they'd be shut down or sold off.

So Welch wasn't just asking for changes at the margins. The

"number one, number two" standard entailed many risks. But if successful, it would position GE for double-digit growth for years to come.

This was only a hint of things to come. Throughout Welch's tenure at GE, he continued to embrace change.

For instance, on December 12, 1985, GE announced plans to purchase communications giant RCA for $6.28 billion.

It was the largest nonoil merger ever. General Electric then ranked ninth on the list of America's largest industrial firms. RCA ranked second among the nation's service firms. Together, they formed a corporate powerhouse with sales of $40 billion, placing it seventh on the Fortune 500.

The purchase represented a sea change for GE. Throughout much of its history, the company had a tradition of growing from within. Welch ignored that tradition. He intended to push General Electric's highest growth businesses and do whatever it took to win.

EMPLOYEES HAVE GOOD IDEAS TOO

At the same time, Welch knew that there were good ideas inside the shop as well. In 1989, he launched an initiative that he called Work-Out, which was an ambitious 10-year program to harness the brains of his employees.

In Welch's words, Work-Out was intended to help people stop:

wrestling with the boundaries, the absurdities, that grow in large organizations. We're all familiar with those absurdities: too many approvals, duplication, pomposity, waste.

Change *worked*. By the 1990s, GE had emerged as the strongest company in America. Yet even that record of achievement did not keep Welch from exploring the next wave of change. In 1995, he took a bold new step and launched a companywide initiative to improve the quality of General Electric's products and processes.

Why? Welch had grown convinced that GE's quality standards simply weren't high enough, even though GE had always been, in his words, a "quality company." So why not stand pat? His answer:

> **We want to be more than that. We want to change the competitive landscape by being not just better than our competitors, but by taking quality to a whole new level. We want to make our quality so special, so valuable to our customers, so important to their success, that our products become their only real value choice.**

An openness to change.

This is Jack Welch's key business strategy:

Change, before it's too late!

WELCH RULES

➤ Accept change. Business leaders who treat change like the enemy will fail at their jobs. Change is the one constant, and successful business leaders must be able to read the ever-changing business environment.

➤ Let your employees know that change never ends. Teach your colleagues to see change as an opportunity—a challenge that can be met through hard work and smarts.

➤ Be ready to rewrite your agenda. Welch always encouraged his managers and employees to be prepared to reexamine their agenda and to make changes when necessary.

LEADERSHIP SECRET 2

FACE REALITY!

FROM THE FILES OF JACK WELCH

The art of leading comes down to one thing: facing reality, and then acting decisively and quickly on that reality.

Jack Welch's goal was to transform GE's businesses into the best in the world. To get there, he devised a strategy called Face Reality.

Welch just couldn't get enough of "facing reality":

It may sound simple, but getting any organization or group of people to see the world the way it is and not the way they wish it were or hope it will be is not as easy as it sounds. We have to permeate every mind in the company with an attitude, with an atmosphere that allows people—in fact, encourages people—to see things as they are, to deal with the way it is now, not the way they wish it would be.

Facing reality in the early 1980s meant taking an entirely new look at GE's businesses and deciding what to do with them. Welch called this process "restructuring."

Restructuring wasn't about change at the margins. It was about scrutinizing the *whole company* and changing things.

IT'S OKAY TO CHANGE A COMPANY

At the core of restructuring was the assumption that it was okay, sometimes even necessary, to change the company.

In October 1981, just 6 months after he took over as CEO, Welch addressed 120 corporate officers and spelled out his agenda. It was nothing short of a revolution.

Bureaucratic waste would come to an end, he said. No longer could anyone write deceptive plans or propose unrealistic budgets. Henceforth, the tough decisions that had to be made *would* be made.

Reading between the lines, Welch was really saying:

Check your old excuses at the door.

Stop insisting that life has been unfair to you. Stop seeing conspiracies. *Deal with situations as they are.* In Welch's words:

> **Most of the mistakes you've made have been through not being willing to face into it, straight in the mirror that reality you find, then taking action right on it.**
>
> **That's all managing is, defining and acting. Not hoping, not waiting for the next plan. Not rethinking it. Getting on with it.**

MOVING QUICKLY

In his later years as CEO at GE, Welch admitted that he himself had not always faced up to reality. Nor had he moved quickly enough to implement major changes at GE:

> **I would have liked to have done things a lot faster. I've been here for 17 years. Imagine if I'd taken 4, 3, or even 1 year too long in making my decisions. I would have had a rude awakening.**

On balance, though, Welch made bold decisions that indicated he was (a) facing reality, (b) adjusting to that reality, and (c) moving quickly.

In the early 1980s, when he realized that GE would have to restructure, he was facing reality: GE needed to devote all of its resources to its strongest businesses.

In the mid-1980s, when he authorized GE's purchase of RCA, he was facing reality: GE needed the acquisition to push high-tech growth.

In the late 1980s, when he began the Work-Out program, he was facing reality: Employees needed a voice in running the company.

In the mid-1990s, when Welch started his now-legendary Six Sigma quality program, he was facing reality: GE's quality programs were just not working.

And in the late 1990s, when the Internet came into its own, Welch faced a new reality. At first, like so many other CEOs, he avoided the Internet. But as new models for doing business in cyberspace emerged, Welch set out to revamp the entire enterprise.

He talked about the Internet, and facing reality, when he addressed GE shareholders in April 2000:

> **Seeing reality for GE in the '80s meant a hard look at a century-old portfolio of business ... Seeing reality today means accepting the fact that e-business is here. It's not coming. It's not the thing of the future. It's *here* ...**

To Jack Welch, facing reality was of supreme importance.

Stick your head in the sand, and your business will stay stuck in the past.

If you face reality and *move quickly*, you have a chance to compete and *win* in a changing business environment.

WELCH RULES

➤ **Face reality.** Business leaders who avoid reality are doomed to failure.

➤ **Act on reality quickly!** Those who truly face reality can't stop there. They must adapt their business strategies to reflect that reality, and they must do so quickly.

➤ **Turn your business around.** Stick your head in the sand, says Welch, and you will fail. Face reality, and you may turn a bad situation into a great one.

LEADERSHIP SECRET 3

MANAGING LESS IS MANAGING BETTER

FROM THE FILES OF JACK WELCH

As we became leaner, we found ourselves communicating better, with fewer interpreters and fewer filters. We found that with fewer layers we had wider spans of management. We weren't managing better. We were managing less, and that was better.

One reason Jack Welch had an enormous impact on the business community was that he headed one of the world's most respected, and most *imitated*, companies. Over the decades, whenever General Electric came up with a new management style, others in American business sought to emulate that style. For example:

- In the 1950s: GE decentralized, and decentralization became the rage.

■ In the 1960s and 1970s: GE created enormous bureaucracies, and largeness became a virtue in the business world.

As these examples suggest, GE managers, in Welch's view, managed far too much. Not so under Welch. He threw out the old rule book and constructed an entirely new set of principles on how to manage.

Or more accurately, how *not* to manage.

Welch argued that managing less was managing better.

THE WELCH PARADOX OF MANAGEMENT

Welch made it very clear that he wanted his managers to manage less. He wanted them to do less monitoring and less supervising and to give their employees more latitude. Conversely, he wanted far *more* decision making at the lower levels of the company.

Obviously, he wasn't suggesting that managers should knock off at noon every day and head for the golf course. Far from it! But he didn't want his managers interfering with their employees at every turn. Instead, he wanted them to concentrate on *creating a vision* for their employees and to make sure that the vision was always on the mark and was being acted upon.

This is counterintuitive, right? Aren't managers supposed to manage? If they manage less, won't the overall performance of the business suffer? Who will make sure employees are working as hard as they can? Who will monitor inventory levels? Who will worry about maintaining the quality of the product?

In addition, managers *want* to manage. They want to keep their fingers on the pulse of the business and keep close tabs on their employees.

Welch responds with one word: *Relax.*

Stop getting in people's way. Cut them some slack. Stop looking over their shoulders. Stop bogging them down in bureaucracy.

Let them *perform.*

SHOW RESPECT, INSTILL CONFIDENCE

Behind this prescription lies a key idea: Your employees deserve respect. You've hired the best people and trained them well, right?

So treat them with respect. Show them you understand that they are doing something important for the company. Build their confidence—in you, in the company, and in themselves.

And then get the hell out of their way.

One welcome by-product of this approach is an increased management focus on the big issues. For Welch, "managing less" at GE meant that his leaders had more time to think big thoughts and be more creative. They gained time to look beyond their own fiefdoms and think about how they might help *other* GE businesses.

As the years wore on, Welch felt that his senior managers were getting better and better at helping one another out. Had these leaders spent large amounts of time firing off memos to their subordinates, checking up on them, or worrying about fine-grain issues, they wouldn't have had the time to devote to the bigger-picture opportunities.

But by managing less, they gained that time and were able to help GE reach the next level.

WELCH RULES

- ➤ **Manage less.** Teach your managers to manage less, even though their training may be to manage more.

- ➤ **Instill confidence.** Treat employees with respect and build their confidence.

- ➤ **Get out of the way.** Employees do not need constant supervision. Let them do their jobs. You will be surprised at the results.

- ➤ **Emphasize vision, not supervision.** Managing less lets managers think big thoughts and come up with new ideas to benefit the business.

LEADERSHIP SECRET 4

CREATE A VISION AND THEN GET OUT OF THE WAY

FROM THE FILES OF JACK WELCH

People always overestimate how complex business is. This isn't rocket science. We've chosen one of the world's simplest professions.

This is one of Jack Welch's fundamental beliefs about management. As he phrases it:

I operate on a very simple belief about business. If there are six of us in a room and we all get the same facts, in most cases the six of us will reach roughly the same conclusion.

The problem is, we don't get the same information. We each get different pieces. Business isn't complicated. The complications arise when people are cut off from information they need.

To get the critical information, Welch says, a manager must ask five key questions:

1. What does your global competitive environment look like?
2. In the last 3 years, what have your competitors done?
3. In the same period, what have you done to them?
4. How might they attack you in the future?
5. What are your plans to leapfrog them?

GE, an enormous enterprise operating on an international scale, is surely a good test of this philosophy. How did Welch manage to keep up with all 12 of GE's businesses? His answer:

> **There are a series of mechanisms that allow you to keep in touch. I travel around the world often, so I'm smelling what people are thinking . . .**
> **None of us runs the businesses. I'm never going to run them. I don't run them at all. If I tried to run them, I'd go crazy. I can smell when someone running [a business] isn't doing it right.**

So again, Welch is more of a "supermanager" than a manager, overseeing a dozen huge businesses simultaneously. He is actively involved but mainly through recruiting talented people, providing vision, and allocating resources.

> **My job is to put the best people on the biggest opportunities, and the best allocation of dollars in the right places.**
> **That's about it. Transfer ideas and allocate resources and get out of the way.**

But information was also critical. Downsizing at GE helped by creating a company that was far more effective at communicating with itself.

> **As we became leaner, we found ourselves communicating better, with fewer interpreters and fewer filters. We found that with fewer layers we had wider spans of management.**

Inevitably, as managers and employees in the lower ranks were asked to take more responsibility, Welch began to feel that it was important to distinguish between leaders and managers:

> **Leaders—and you take anyone from Roosevelt to Churchill to Reagan—inspire people with clear visions of how things can be done better. Some managers, on the other hand, muddle things with pointless complexity and detail. They equate [managing] with sophistication, with sounding smarter than anyone else. They inspire no one.**

Jack Welch never involved himself in deciding on the style of a refrigerator or what television programs NBC should schedule for Thursday night prime time. As he put it:

> **I have no idea how to produce a good [television] program and just as little about how to build an engine . . . But I do know who the boss at NBC is. And that is what matters. It is my job to choose the best people and to provide them with the dollars. That's how the game is played.**

What companies and business leaders must do, he argues, is to

> **provide an atmosphere, a climate, a chance, a meritocracy, where people can have the resources to grow, the educational tools are available, they can expand their horizons, their vision of life. That's what companies ought to provide . . .**
>
> **People say to me, "Aren't you afraid of losing control? You're not measuring [anymore]." We couldn't lose control of this place. We've got 106 years of people measuring everything. So we're not going to lose control. It's in our blood.**

WELCH RULES

➤ Business is simple. Complications arise when people are cut off from vital information.

➤ Always keep the five key questions in mind: What does your global competitive environment look like? In the last 3 years, what have your competitors done?

In the same period, what have you done to them? How might they attack you in the future? What are your plans to leapfrog them?

➤ **Managing is allocating people and resources.** Put the right people in the right job, give them what they need, and then get out of the way.

➤ **Managers lead with vision.** Managers must persuade others to implement through the force of vision.

LEADERSHIP
SECRET 5

DON'T PURSUE A CENTRAL IDEA; INSTEAD, SET ONLY A FEW CLEAR, GENERAL GOALS AS BUSINESS STRATEGIES

FROM THE FILES OF JACK WELCH

I am not going to attempt, for the sake of intellectual neatness, to tie a bow around the many diverse initiatives of General Electric.

At the end of his first year as CEO, Jack Welch explained what he wanted to do at GE:

> If I could, this would be the appropriate moment for me to withdraw from my pocket a sealed envelope containing the grand strategy for the General Electric Company over the next decade. But I can't . . .

> **What will enhance the many decentralized plans and initiatives of this company isn't a central strategy, but a central idea—a simple core concept that will guide General Electric in the '80s and govern our diverse plans and strategies.**

Instead of directing GE's businesses on the basis of a specific step-by-step strategic plan, Welch preferred to set out only a few clear, general goals. This would permit his employees to make the most of opportunities that came their way.

Welch was impressed by what he had read about the Prussian military strategists in the nineteenth century:

> **They did not expect a plan of operation to survive beyond the first contact with the enemy. They set only the broadest of objectives and emphasized seizing unforeseen opportunities as they arose.**

In running GE, Welch adopted the same attitude: Strategy would not be etched in stone but instead would evolve over time. It was important to set broad objectives that were consistent with the company's values and to apply those values as situations arose.

The values that guided Welch through the 1980s and 1990s were very general. But taken together, they provided a strong management framework:

- Create a clear, simple, reality-based, customer-focused vision and be able to communicate it in a straightforward way to all constituencies.

- Understand accountability and commitment and be decisive; set and meet aggressive targets; always with unyielding integrity.

- Have a passion for excellence; hate bureaucracy and all the nonsense that comes with it.

- Have the self-confidence to empower others and behave in a boundaryless fashion; believe in and be committed to Work-Out as a means of empowerment; be open to ideas from anywhere.

- Have, or have the capacity to develop, global brains and global sensitivity, and be comfortable building diverse global teams. Stimulate and relish change; do not be frightened or paralyzed by it. See change as opportunity, not just a threat.

- Have enormous energy and the ability to energize and invigorate others. Understand speed as a competitive advantage.

To show the consistency of Welch's attitude toward change at GE over the years, we include a version of those values from the summer of 2000.

GE leaders . . . always with unyielding integrity:

- Are passionately focused on driving customer success

- Live Six Sigma quality, ensure that the customer is always its first beneficiary, and use it to accelerate growth

- Insist on excellence and are intolerant of bureaucracy

- Act in a boundaryless fashion; always search for and apply the best ideas regardless of their source

- Prize global intellectual capital and the people that provide it; build diverse teams to maximize it

- See change for the growth opportunities it brings, e.g., e-business

- Create a clear, simple, customer-centered vision, and continually renew and refresh its execution

- Create an environment of "stretch," excitement, informality, and trust; reward improvements and celebrate results

- Demonstrate, always with infectious enthusiasm for the customer, the 4-E's of GE leadership: the personal Energy to welcome and deal with the speed of change, the ability to create an atmosphere that Energizes others, the Edge to make difficult decisions, and the ability to consistently Execute

Don't get bogged down in details, Welch advises. Lay out your goals and adjust to changing realities as you go along.

WELCH RULES

➤ **Set out a general framework for your team.** Do not try to set a detailed game plan for every situation.

➤ **Create values that are consistent with the company vision.** Values should reflect the vision, culture, and goals of the organization.

➤ **Make sure there is room to maneuver.** Core values should be constant, but the strategies may need to change with the competitive environment.

LEADERSHIP SECRET 6

NURTURE EMPLOYEES WHO SHARE THE COMPANY'S VALUES

FROM THE FILES OF JACK WELCH

The hardest thing in the world is to move against somebody who is delivering the goods but acting 180 degrees from [your values]. But if you don't act, you're not walking the talk and you're just an air bag.

Welch has often summarized his thoughts on the essential traits of an effective manager. In his first such effort, he described four categories:

A. *Delivers on commitments—financial or otherwise—and shares GE's values.* "His or her future is an easy call," says Welch. "Onward and upward."

B. *Does not meet commitments and does not share GE's values.* "Not as pleasant a call, but equally easy."

C. *Misses commitments but shares the values.* "He or she usually gets a second chance, preferably in a different environment."

D. *Delivers on commitments but does not subscribe to GE's values.* What happens to managers who deliver the numbers but do not live the GE values? According to Welch, they get fired.

That's a shell shock to our company, because numbers are no longer job security. Values and numbers now mean job security.

KEEP THE A'S; GET RID OF THE C'S

By January 1997, Welch was using different language to make the same points. Speaking to the company's top 500 managers, he urged his colleagues to work hard to hang on to the "category A's"—in other words, the team players who subscribed to the company's values. He urged that they also nurture the B's but move quickly to get rid of the C's:

Too many of you work too hard to make C's [into] B's. It is a wheel-spinning exercise. Push C's on to B companies or C companies, and they'll do just fine...

Take care of your best. Reward them. Promote them. Pay them well. Give them a lot of [stock] options and don't spend all that time trying work plans to get C's to be B's. Move them on out early. It's a contribution.

Eight months later, Welch spoke again about the characteristics of A, B, and C managers. He told managers that the key was to demand more of the A's, to cultivate them, and to nourish them. The best thing to do with the C's, he said again, was to *get rid of them.*

Someone in the audience confessed that she had recently been forced to let some people go and that she felt bad about it. Welch replied without hesitation: *Don't feel guilty.*

Callous? Not to Welch. As he saw it, it was simply good business.

As Welch watched the business environment grow much more competitive and intense in the late 1990s, he concluded that being a business leader had become far more demanding.

> **The thing I've noticed is that the intensity level and the global understanding and the facing reality and the seeing the world as it is, is so much more pronounced in December 1997 than it was 10 years ago, and certainly 15 years ago, where form was very important...**
>
> **Global battles don't allow form. It's all substance. Form means somebody is not intensely interested in the company.**

Welch likes to say that 20 years ago, being named CEO of a company was the culmination of a career. But today's CEO must think of stepping into the top job as only the beginning of the real battles:

> **No one can come to work and sit, no one can go off and think of just policy, no one can do any of these things. You've got to be live action all day. And you've got to be able to energize others.... You've got to be on the lunatic fringe.**

What does all this add up to? For one thing, it means surrounding yourself with category A's—that is, the *best possible people*:

> **The biggest advice I give people is you cannot do these jobs alone. You've got to be very comfortable with the brightest human beings alive on your team. And if you do that, you get the world by the tail...**
>
> **Always get the best people. If you [don't], you're shortchanging yourself.**

WELCH RULES

➤ Give employees more responsibility, and they will make better decisions. By making your employees more accountable, you make your organization more productive.

➤ Nurture the employees who live up to company values, even if they don't make their numbers. Consider reassigning them if their numbers continue to falter.

➤ Eliminate employees who do not live the company values, even if their numbers are good. Difficult, yes, but absolutely necessary.

PART II

IGNITING A REVOLUTION:
STRATEGIES FOR DEALING WITH CHANGE

LEADERSHIP SECRET 7

KEEP WATCH FOR WAYS TO CREATE OPPORTUNITIES AND TO BECOME MORE COMPETITIVE

FROM THE FILES OF JACK WELCH

The world is moving at such a pace that control has become a limitation. It slows you down.

Before Jack Welch's arrival at GE, the company was steaming full throttle toward the cliff edge.

Yes, the balance sheet was strong. But only a handful of the company's 350 business units dominated their markets. The only GE businesses doing well on a global basis were plastics, gas turbines, and aircraft engines (and overseas, only gas turbines were dominant). Something like 80 percent of GE's earnings still came from its traditional electrical and electronic manufacturing businesses at a time when the manufacturing sector was nose-diving. A number of GE's businesses—aircraft engines, for one—often consumed more cash than they generated.

There *were* success stories such as financial services, medical systems, and plastics. But these businesses contributed only one-third to total corporate earnings in 1981.

GE's ADVERSARIES

GE's adversaries were a changing global business environment and a weakening domestic economy.

For much of the twentieth century, America had dominated the most important markets of the world economy: steel, textiles, shipbuilding, television, calculators, automobiles.

Gradually, though, the competitive arena shifted. The Japanese, in particular, began to lure clients away with higher-quality, lower-cost products. To compete for business around the world, the United States would have to become far more productive.

But by the early 1980s, the American economy was increasingly unhealthy. Inflation, only 3.4 percent in 1971, had soared to 18 percent in March 1980. (One culprit was the price of oil, which spiked from $1.70 per barrel in 1971 to $39 per barrel in 1980.) As Jack Welch assumed the reins at GE in the spring of 1981, the American economy was mired in the deepest recession in a half-century.

Welch's business ideas were formed as a response to these fundamental changes in the global business environment. He understood, better than most, that the business arena had become increasingly competitive. He had watched a whole new array of enterprises with international capabilities pop up around the globe. He understood that a completely new vision was required and, along with that new vision, a new set of business strategies.

THE MOST COMPETITIVE ENTERPRISE ON EARTH

Jack Welch had a gut feeling that something required fixing.

> **I could see a lot of [GE] businesses becoming . . . lethargic. American business was inwardly focused on the bureaucracy.**
>
> **[That bureaucracy] was right for its time, but the times were changing rapidly. Change was occurring at a much faster pace than business was reacting to it.**

Many in American business believed that layer upon layer of management created the tightest possible command-and-control system and, therefore, the best operations. But to Welch, those layers wasted precious time and resources and distracted the company.

> **The old organization was built on control, but the world has changed . . . You've got to balance freedom with some control, but you've got to have more freedom than you ever dreamed of.**

What was Jack Welch's vision? Simply this: To make General Electric the most competitive enterprise on earth. As he told shareholders on his first day in office:

> **A decade from now we would like General Electric to be perceived as a unique, high-spirited, entrepreneurial enterprise . . . a company known around the world for its unmatched level of excellence. We want General Electric to be the most profitable, highly diversified company on earth, with world-quality leadership in every one of its product lines.**

He could not wait to put his business ideas to work—to test them, to find out which were valid and which were not. He would shape and refine his ideas. He was determined to make good on his promise to grow GE into the most successful business enterprise in America.

WELCH RULES

➤ **Don't stick your head in the sand.** From the start, Welch had his finger on the pulse of the competitive environment. Keep a close tab on those key variables that create opportunities and challenges for your business.

➤ **See things for what they are.** Allocate resources to market-leading businesses, fix ailing companies, and jettison those that are not competitive.

➤ **Begin with a vision.** Nothing changes without a clear vision of where change is supposed to lead. The boldest vision may be the best vision.

LEADERSHIP
SECRET 8

BE NUMBER ONE OR NUMBER TWO AND KEEP REDEFINING YOUR MARKET

There will be no room for the mediocre supplier of products and services—the company in the middle of the pack.

In the early 1980s, Jack Welch decided to pursue a strategy that would establish each of the company's businesses as either number one or number two in its market.

He warned that without such a strategy, the company's prospects would be dim.

The winners in this slow-growth environment will be those who search out and participate in the real growth industries and insist upon being number one or number two in every

business they are in . . . or those who have a clear technological edge, a clear advantage in a market niche.

Welch was establishing literally the highest possible standards for his businesses. He made it clear that he would accept nothing less.

SETTING THE BAR AS HIGH AS POSSIBLE

Given the large portfolio of businesses that he presided over, Welch felt he needed a breakaway strategy that would create a "survival of the fittest" mindset throughout the company.

GE's managers, said Welch, now had to ask some difficult questions:

> **Where we are not number one or number two, and don't have or can't see a route to a technological edge, we have got to ask ourselves [management theorist] Peter Drucker's very tough question: "If you weren't already in the business, would you enter it today?" And if the answer is no, face into that second difficult question: "What are you going to do about it?"**

Within the company, there was widespread unhappiness. "Why was it necessary to be number one or two?" anxious managers asked. What was wrong with being a solid number three or four?

In response, Welch pointed out that in many markets, it was the number three, four, five, or six businesses that suffered the most during cyclical downturns. Number one or two businesses could defend their market share either through aggressive pricing strategies or the development of new products. Runners-up could not.

Moreover, Welch argued, many managers who believed they were third or fourth in their markets were mistaken because they were considering only their domestic competition. When international competitors were factored in, they were likely to fall far lower in the "rankings."

Citing his own experience, Welch explained the difference between a market leader and an also-ran:

> **I ran some businesses that were number one or two and some businesses that were four or five, so I had the luxury of a laboratory...And it was clear to me that one was a helluva lot easier and better than the other one. The other one didn't have the resources and the muscle and the power to compete on a global scale that was emerging in the '90s.**

But the skeptics persisted. "Why sell off a business," they asked, "when it's making good money?" Again, Welch had an answer.

> **When you're number four or five in a market, when number one sneezes, you get pneumonia. When you're number one, you control your destiny.**

One problem quickly presented itself. The company was producing a wide variety of seemingly unrelated products, from time-shares to nuclear reactors to microwave ovens. Could GE excel in so many different areas?

The answer turned out to be yes. By 2000, GE had achieved dominance or near dominance in dozens of markets across the globe:

- Number one in the world: industrial motors, medical systems, plastics, financial services, transport, power generation, information services, aircraft engines, and electric distribution equipment. NBC, which includes general-interest programming (and its CNBC business-news offshoot), was ranked the number one American network.

- Number two in the world: lighting and household appliances.

ADJUSTING THE STRATEGY

So Number One, Number Two was a big win. By the mid-1990s, however, it was clear that the strategy had its limitations.

For one thing, it was vulnerable to GE managers defining markets in ways that benefited them. GE managers learned to define their markets in ways that *guaranteed* an outcome of number one or two, often by defining their own markets far too narrowly.

For example, GE's power-generation business developed products for the large utilities and defined its market as "large power plants." But by so doing, the division neglected the increasingly important distributed-power market.

Welch ordered the strategy revised in early 1996. The refinement came at an opportune time: just as GE was planning to expand its service offerings. For example, for years, GE had serviced only GE aircraft engines. In 1997, however, it expanded the business and started to offer repair and parts for Pratt & Whitney and Rolls Royce engines.

Might redefining these markets make it more difficult for divisions to retain their hard-won number one or number two positions? Temporarily, perhaps. But Welch insisted that he would stay the course as long as he was convinced that the company was (a) building on strengths and (b) had the opportunity to be number one.

By revising the Number One, Number Two strategy, Welch faced reality, embraced change, shook things up, and forced his key managers to scrutinize their businesses all over again.

WELCH RULES

➤ **Develop market-leading businesses.** Number one and number two businesses can withstand downturns, but laggards fall further behind when times get tough.

➤ **Define markets broadly.** Don't make the mistake of defining markets so narrowly that you shut yourself out of growing market segments.

LEADERSHIP SECRET 9

DOWNSIZE, BEFORE IT'S TOO LATE!

FROM THE FILES OF JACK WELCH

These are the businesses that we really want to nourish. These are the businesses that will take us into the twenty-first century. They are inside the circles. Outside the circles you have businesses that we would prefer not to pursue any further.

Jack Welch felt he had no choice. He not only had to reshape the company but also reduce its size dramatically.

Alone among American business leaders, Welch was willing to downsize a company that was not facing an imminent crisis. He knew this would be a heart-wrenching process. But the result would be worth it: a GE that was sleek, aggressive, and competitive.

DOWNSIZING: AN UPHILL BATTLE

Prior to the 1980s, conventional wisdom decreed that employees should be let go only as a last resort and only when a company was on the brink of a major business reversal.

So when "downsizing" first appeared on the American business landscape, it was taken as an indication of a serious decline in the downsizing company's fortunes. Or perhaps worse, it was seen as an evasion of corporate social responsibility.

Apart from that, it was difficult to fire people.

One principle that labor unions had hammered into the American consciousness was the right of every individual to hold a job. To some extent, this translated into a right not to be fired.

Meanwhile, the politicians in Washington had accepted the notion that jobs, especially in one's home district, were more important than a corporation's bottom line.

And for their part, corporate managers had little appetite for firing employees. Some didn't want to make the tough decisions. Others believed in the principle of job security, arguing that it fostered loyalty and productivity.

Jack Welch, however, believed that lifetime employment was a failed strategy. GE's competition in the early 1980s was coming from foreign firms whose workers had achieved higher productivity rates. To compete with those companies, GE would have to invest in new equipment and cut payrolls.

Welch's position constituted a dramatic shift in corporate thinking. In 1981, GE rang up profits of $1.5 billion, and the company didn't appear to be in trouble. The effect of Welch's downsizing program would be to put thousands of GE employees out of work. His tactics soon made him one of the most controversial CEOs in America.

It was an uphill battle and no doubt a lonely one. No other American CEO reached the decision to perform radical surgery on his or her own company, even before conclusive evidence of a life-threatening illness had emerged. Welch stood alone.

THE NICKNAME HE HATES

The reactions to Welch's initial efforts at restructuring were highly negative. He was dubbed "Neutron Jack"—an allusion to the neutron bomb, which kills people but leaves buildings standing.

Neutron Jack: The name haunted Welch.

The media used it to characterize him as a heartless, evil individual—a manager who cared only for the bottom line and not for the good of his employees.

Welch's bitterness is clear as he talks about his hated nickname:

> **I think it was a harsh term. Mean-spirited. They call me "Neutron Jack" because we laid off people even though we gave them the best benefits they had in their life.**

Despite all the controversy, it wasn't a close call in Welch's mind. He was convinced that only massive surgery would ensure GE's long-term success.

He did not think that he had a choice.

He was not at the helm of GE to make his employees happy.

He was there to make the company as profitable as possible.

WELCH RULES

➤ **Even in the good times, regularly review expenses and head counts.** Welch downsized when GE appeared to be healthy. Don't assume that because all is well at the moment, it will stay that way. (And are you *sure* all is well?)

➤ **Don't lead by polls.** CEOs should not run companies as if they were popularity contests. Welch didn't hesitate to make himself unpopular in his early years, bucking conventions and conventional wisdom. Do what you know is right for the long-term health of the organization.

➤ **Remember that tough actions today may prevent far more complex problems later.** Had Welch not restructured in the early 1980s, he might have had to eliminate far more jobs in later years.

LEADERSHIP SECRET 10

USE ACQUISITIONS TO MAKE
THE QUANTUM LEAP!

FROM THE FILES OF JACK WELCH

*This [acquisition of Honeywell] is the most exciting deal for GE since RCA ... the success of the RCA deal—which was probably one of the most successful deals in corporate history—will bode well for this one. ...
We're merging two real high-tech companies. With real earnings. Doing real things.*

—Jack Welch, October 2000

Call it a surprise move.
    Call it the tactic that turns an above-average company into a superstar.

Call it the bold ploy that you spring while others sit stunned, unable to counter your adventurous gambit.

Surprise, boldness, and even shock—these are the features of the quantum leap.

Going for the quantum leap is what Welch had in mind when he launched the two largest acquisitions in GE's history: RCA in 1985 and Honeywell in 2000. And although GE was ultimately frustrated in its bid for Honeywell, the gambit can hold interesting lessons.

Welch's goal, in both cases, was not simply to make the company bigger. His goal was to build up GE's highest growth businesses and thereby grow earnings. Acquiring businesses that could add to GE's earnings became a hallmark of the new Welch-driven culture.

THE FIRST QUANTUM LEAP

Welch first cast a covetous eye on RCA, the Radio Corporation of America, in the mid-1980s.

Like GE, RCA was one of America's most famous corporate names. RCA had interests in defense electronics, consumer electronics, and satellites. But the jewel in RCA's crown was the National Broadcasting Company (NBC), which it had created in 1926.

Until Welch made his move, the three major television networks had seemed untouchable. Most people assumed that their owners would never part with these highly profitable "trophy" properties.

Not Welch. Sometime in 1984, Welch began pondering a GE-RCA merger. General Electric in 1984 had sales of $27.9 billion, and RCA had just over $10 billion. Together, they would constitute a new corporate powerhouse that would rank seventh on the Fortune 500.

Welch was convinced that the merger would augment GE's drive into the service and technology fields and reduce its dependence on slow-growth manufacturing businesses.

The deal, announced December 12, 1985, was Jack Welch's

boldest move to that point. GE and RCA agreed that General Electric would buy the communications giant for $6.28 billion, or $66.50 a share—the largest nonoil merger ever. Since Wall Street analysts valued RCA at $90 per share, GE appeared to have gotten a very good deal, indeed.

"This is going to be one dynamite company," Welch said happily. "We will have the technological capabilities, financial resources, and global scope to be able to compete successfully with anyone, anywhere, in every market we serve . . ."

Welch particularly enjoyed the spark he found among NBC entertainment executives. "They're our type of people. They know how to be number one." As a result of Welch's audacity, General Electric was now a very different company.

THE SECOND QUANTUM LEAP

Even as he was preparing to retire in the fall of 2000, Welch came upon an opportunity to make another quantum leap. Honeywell International, Welch's new target, was a manufacturer of aerospace systems, power and transportation products, specialty chemicals, home security systems, and building controls.

Honeywell seemed like a great fit with GE. Both companies made power-generation systems, plastics, and chemicals. GE aircraft engines were a major force in the commercial aircraft field; Honeywell was strong in avionics and business jet engines.

If the Honeywell deal went through, it would add $24 billion to GE's annual revenues of $112 billion. GE's profits—already on the order of $11 billion a year—would grow by another $2.5 billion.

On October 23, 2000, GE and Honeywell announced that GE would purchase Honeywell for $48.4 billion in stock and assumed debt. GE would acquire another 120,000 employees, giving the expanded General Electric a payroll of 460,000. "I want an apology from everybody that ever called me Neutron Jack," Welch said pointedly. "We have more people today than we did when I started."

But Welch was not pleased when some wondered out loud why GE had chosen to buy a so-called "Old Economy company."

> **My answer is: What the hell do you think Honeywell is? ...We're merging two real high-tech companies. With real earnings. Doing real things. And using e-business tools. So get that straight.**

Buying Honeywell made sense, Welch argued, because there was a 90 percent overlap between the two companies.

> **And yet with virtually every single activity there is no product overlap. So the feels are the same in 90 percent of the businesses and yet everything is complementary. That's not a speech for the antitrust people. That's fact ...**

Welch had reason to be concerned about antitrust actions. Merging the two corporate giants was sure to attract intense governmental scrutiny. And at first, things went well. In May 2001, the U.S. Department of Justice approved the transaction. (Canada and nearly a dozen other jurisdictions followed suit.) But 2 months later, the European Commission demanded concessions that Welch couldn't accept. "What the Commission is seeking cuts the heart out of the strategic rationale of our deal," Welch wrote in a letter to Honeywell CEO Michael R. Bonsignore.

The deal was dead.

THE "HIDDEN" QUANTUM LEAP

While the Honeywell deal was still alive, Welch announced his intention to delay his retirement from GE to ensure that the merger went smoothly. Critics suggested that he had contrived the Honeywell deal just to stay on longer at GE. Ridiculous, he responded:

> This is *not* a story of the old fool who can't leave his seat
> ... Don't write that story. That story is stupid. In the paper, I
> called it "B" with a bunch of dashes ... Why not take advan-
> tage of the experience I've got with RCA and over a thousand
> other acquisitions?

In this response, Welch points to what might be considered GE's hidden "quantum leap": the patient acquisition over 20 years of numerous companies, all designed to propel GE toward higher sales and earnings.

Under Welch, GE was constantly on the lookout for small companies that could be quickly integrated into the company's units and which would immediately add to earnings. In 1999 alone, for example, GE closed *125* of these deals. The $48 billion, or $55 a share, Welch offered for Honeywell was half as much as all the deals GE had done under his watch combined.

The result? A company that in 2000 operated in more than 100 countries and earned revenues of *$130 billion.*

WELCH RULES

➤ Go for the quantum leap, even if it goes against company culture. When Welch acquired RCA, he rewrote
GE's rule book.

➤ Think outside the box. Both the RCA and Honeywell
deals were audacious moves. One panned out; the
other didn't.

➤ Keep hunting for the little opportunities. The big,
bold moves need to be part of a patient, systematic
approach to mergers and acquisitions.

LEADERSHIP SECRET 11

LEARNING CULTURE I: USE BOUNDARYLESSNESS AND EMPOWERMENT TO NURTURE A LEARNING CULTURE

FROM THE FILES OF JACK WELCH

The operative assumption today is that some-one, somewhere, has a better idea.

Before Jack Welch came along, many analysts thought GE to be unmanageably huge, complex, and heterogeneous. Some considered the company a rudderless conglomerate—a collection of assets that lacked coherence and a unifying vision.

Welch did not agree.

He believed that GE's diversity and complexity could be

turned into an asset if he could create what he called a "learning culture." In a learning culture, GE's employees would search for new ideas—inside or outside the company—and implement the best ones actively and aggressively.

Large and diverse corporations, as Welch saw it, have contradictory needs. They need both strong integration and rich diversity. In combination, these two ingredients enable the whole to outperform the sum of its parts. Welch referred to this as "integrated diversity," and this was his goal.

OPENNESS IS ESSENTIAL

Learning organizations, said Welch, have an edge. Learning translates into actions, and actions spark productivity.

The idea of the learning culture was simple: GE businesses would share knowledge from every corner of the company.

Shared knowledge would provide a competitive advantage, and that advantage would translate into higher annual growth rates.

Welch observed that integrated diversity could work only when the component parts of that diversity—GE's businesses— were strong in their own right. That was why it had been so important to create strong, stand-alone businesses in the 1980s. From strength came self-confidence, and from self-confidence came openness.

Openness, Welch said, was essential.

LEARNING CULTURE ENHANCES PERFORMANCE

How do you build a learning culture? The Work-Out program of the early 1990s set the stage. At the heart of Work-Out was the assumption that in many cases employees knew what was best. As Welch noted:

> The operative assumption today is that someone, some-
> where, has a better idea; and the operative compulsion is to
> find out who has that better idea, learn it, and put it into ac-
> tion—fast.
> The quality of an idea does not depend on its altitude in
> the organization ... An idea can be from any source. So we
> will search the globe for ideas. We will share what we know
> with others to get what they know. We have a constant quest
> to raise the bar, and we get there by constantly talking to
> others.

Welch was fond of saying that GE's core competence lay in
sharing ideas across businesses, across what he termed the
"boundaryless organization." He wanted GE to think of itself as
a series of laboratories that shared ideas, financial resources, and
managers. He encouraged a free flow of ideas not just among
GE businesses but also between GE and other companies as well.

Speaking to GE shareholders in April 2000, Welch reempha-
sized his commitment to the learning culture. The ultimate, sus-
tainable competitive advantage of a company, he proclaimed, is
its ability to learn, to transfer that learning across its components, and to *act quickly*:

> That belief drove us to create a boundaryless company by
> delayering and destroying organizational silos. Selflessly
> sharing good ideas while endlessly searching for better ideas
> became a natural act. We purged NIH—not invented here—
> from our system, creating a company with an insatiable de-
> sire for information.
> All this was done the hard way, before the arrival of the
> Internet. Today, with the Internet, information is available
> everywhere to everyone, and a company that isn't searching
> for the best idea, isn't open to ideas from anywhere, will find
> itself left behind, with its survival at stake.

The result? Welch credited GE's learning culture with en-
hancing the company's performance in several ways:

■ Operating margins, less than 10 percent for literally a
   century, rose to 17.3 percent in 1999.

■ Inventory turns, which are a key measure of how well assets are deployed and managed, had run in the three to four range for a century but topped eight in 1999.

■ Company earnings, which had shown only single-digit increases throughout the 1980s, showed double-digit increases for most of the 1990s.

WELCH RULES

➤ **Emphasize idea sharing inside the company.** Does your company have a way to make sure ideas are exchanged at every level and from every corner of the company?

➤ **Find and implement the best ideas, no matter where they come from.** Welch demolished the notion that the best ideas come only from within.

➤ **Make sure that great ideas are followed by implementation.** Unless the idea is acted on, it will have little impact.

LEADERSHIP
SECRET 12

LEARNING CULTURE II: INCULCATE THE BEST IDEAS INTO THE BUSINESS, NO MATTER WHERE THEY COME FROM

We really view ourselves as a series of laboratories that share ideas, financial resources, and management people.

K*eep learning*: This is one of the anchors of Jack Welch's business philosophy.

Don't be arrogant, he insists. Don't assume you know it all. Always assume that you can learn from someone else.

From a colleague, for example, or even from a competitor. *Especially* from a competitor!

SCOUR THE LANDSCAPE

Welch exhorted his troops to scour the corporate landscape for good ideas and then to appropriate those ideas. "Legitimate plagiarism" he once called it: borrowing the best.

Some might wonder why GE—arguably one of the strongest companies in the United States—needs to go hunting for good ideas. Shouldn't GE be teaching other companies what business is all about?

Absolutely not, says Welch. Every organization has to learn, and GE is no exception.

Here is Welch on the subject:

> **At the heart of this culture is an understanding that an organization's ability to learn, and translate that learning into action rapidly, is the ultimate competitive business advantage.**

THE BADGE OF HONOR

It is a true badge of honor, according to Welch, to grab good ideas and run with them.

This kind of opportunism begins at home. Welch likes to point out that GE businesses share many things such as technology, design, personnel compensation and evaluation systems, manufacturing processes, and customer and country knowledge. The gas turbines business shares manufacturing technology with aircraft engines. Motors and transportation systems work together on new locomotive-propulsion systems.

But the learning continues beyond the walls of GE. For example, GE has adopted and adapted new product-introduction techniques from Chrysler and Canon, effective sourcing techniques from GM and Toyota, and quality initiatives from Motorola and Ford.

Note that by definition GE isn't "first" with these ideas. GE did not invent the Six Sigma quality initiative. (Motorola pioneered it.) GE wasn't even the next large company to get on board. (AlliedSignal was an early adapter.) But GE watched Six Sigma go through its shakedown cruises at other companies and then adapted it for its own purposes.

A large company like GE has access to a whole world of ideas, but the only way to turn that access into a competitive advantage is to develop what Welch calls a "pervasive and insatiable thirst" for those ideas, a compulsion to share them, and a mandate to implement them.

> **These are our three ingredients for success, whether the business is appliances, lighting, plastics, or something else: Build a good team, share ideas across businesses, give them resources to go. That's it.**

MOVING IDEAS: A KEY TO A LEARNING CULTURE

Moving ideas, Welch likes to say, is easy—assuming you have a learning culture.

One favorite Welch example of the learning culture in action came from its medical systems business, which created a CT scanner that operated remotely. The scanner allowed a user to detect and repair an impending malfunction on-line, often before the customer even knew a problem existed.

Medical systems shared that technology with other GE businesses, including jet engines, locomotives, motors and industrial systems, and power systems. Using the new tool, those other GE businesses could monitor the performance of jet engines, locomotives, paper mills, and power plants.

Welch was once asked how knowledge was transferred among the various GE businesses. He noted that every quarter some 30 GE managers hold a 2-day meeting. Each executive stands up in turn and presents new ideas:

When we leave there after 48 hours, we may not be the smartest people in the world, but we are the most knowledgeable at that moment, because we have been exposed to all these relevant topics....

Most organizations don't go for ideas in a meeting. Why not? Because everybody present comes from the same business. They talk about the vertical business. We talk about compensation plans, about China, about generic experiences.

Building a learning culture has put pressure on GE's business leaders. They understand there is no reward for simply *having* a good idea at GE. The rewards come from successfully sharing that idea with others.

WELCH RULES

➤ Make searching for new ideas a priority of every employee. In today's competitive environment, organizations can't afford to leave anyone out.

➤ Hold idea-sharing meetings on a regular basis. Get a diverse group of managers together regularly. Make sure their ideas are translated into action.

➤ Reward employees for sharing knowledge. Find a way to reward managers and employees for sharing ideas and putting best practices to work at every level.

LEADERSHIP SECRET 13

THE BIG WINNERS IN THE TWENTY-FIRST CENTURY WILL BE GLOBAL

FROM THE FILES OF JACK WELCH

The idea of a company being global is nonsense. Businesses are global, not companies.

From the time Jack Welch became CEO at GE, he was convinced that significant opportunities existed for company growth by taking its businesses overseas.

OVERCOMING INERTIA

In the early 1980s, few U.S. managers were pushing to globalize. Their businesses had prospered by concentrating on the American market; few saw any compelling reason to change.

The pre-Welch GE, which generated more than 80 percent of its revenues in the United States, was no exception. At that time, only two of GE's strategic businesses (plastics and aircraft engines) were legitimate global enterprises.

Welch delayed his push into the international arena for several years—while the company went through its "fix, sell, or close" phase—and then he pushed with a vengeance.

By 1999, international revenues had reached $45.7 billion, representing *41 percent* of GE's total revenues. (The figure remained at 41 percent through 2001.)

THE FORMULA

How did this transformation happen?

In part, it happened the old-fashioned way: through selective, ground-up investments intended to capitalize on local business opportunities.

This reflected Welch's own experiences in the plastics business in the 1960s:

> **When I was 29 years old, I bought land in Holland and built the plants there. That was "my land" for "my business." I was never interested in the global GE, just the global plastics business . . . the idea of a company being global is nonsense.**

This perception reinforced Welch's determination to look for overseas markets with the greatest near-term opportunities. At the time, this was Europe and Japan. Welch was eager to enter other markets in Asia, but he understood that in the near term, those markets were smaller, and success would come more slowly.

So Europe was a clear focus. As of September 1999, GE had paid nearly $30 billion for 133 European acquisitions with 90,000 employees. As a result, GE Europe generated $24.4 billion in revenue, of which only $1.7 billion, or 11 percent, represented imports from the United States. (By 2001, GE had $26 billion in sales in Europe with 70,000 employees in that sector.)

But the transformation also grew out of a major shift in corporate mindsets, beginning with Welch himself.

"Jack's perception of the world changed in the late 1980s," says Gary Wendt, former head of GE Capital, "from trying to sell things to the world to understanding that GE has to be all over the world in order to sell around the world."

Inevitably, this meant that good ideas had to come from places other than the United States. And it explains the major step that GE took at the end of the 1990s:

> **Our insatiable appetite for more advanced technology is being fed not by a new wing on our world-class Corporate R&D Center in Schenectady, New York, but by a soon-to-open Greenfield laboratory in the suburbs of Bangalore, India.**

The Bangalore R&D facility opened in September 2000. And it was only a piece of a bigger picture. By that time, GE was drawing on intellectual capital from all over the world: from metallurgists in Prague to product designers in Budapest, Monterrey, Tokyo, Paris, and elsewhere.

A "TRULY GLOBAL" GE

As a result of these changes, GE by the late 1990s was competing successfully in markets around the world. To cite just three examples:

- *Aircraft Engines.* In 1995, more than half of the world's large commercial jet engine orders were awarded to GE and its joint venture, CFM International.

- *Capital Services.* GE Capital Services, which had a minimal presence in Europe at the start of the 1990s, exceeded $845 million in net income in 1999. Global Consumer Finance (GCF), launched in 1992, emerged as the largest international consumer finance company in the world, with more than $35 billion in assets and more than 20,000 employees.

- *Lighting.* GE Lighting's operations include joint ventures in China, Indonesia, India, and Japan and acquisitions in the United Kingdom, Germany, Italy, and Hungary. As of 1999, more than 35 percent of Lighting's revenues came from outside the United States.

Welch pointed out in his 1999 annual report that there were fewer and fewer American GE business leaders located outside the United States. Local leaders, trained in GE's practices and values, were replacing them.

> **Our objective is to be the "global employer of choice."** . . .
> **This initiative has taken us to within reach of one of our biggest and longest running dreams—a truly global GE.**

WELCH RULES

➤ **Get your house in order first.** Make sure your domestic base is solid before venturing abroad.

➤ **Think globally and locally.** To compete in the global economy, companies must develop a distinct strategy for each international market. Businesses, not companies, are global.

➤ **Recognize that there are phases in globalization.** Exporting often comes first. Local production may come second. Finally, local sourcing (by companies run by local managers) may be your third phase of globalization.

PART III

REMOVING THE BOSS ELEMENT:
PRODUCTIVITY SECRETS FOR CREATING THE
BOUNDARYLESS ORGANIZATION

LEADERSHIP SECRET 14

DELAYER: GET RID OF THE FAT!

FROM THE FILES OF JACK WELCH

Every layer is a bad layer. Now we don't have all that nonsense. If Delhi wants something, they fax me. It's much easier.

Most of Welch's early moves at GE—downsizing; number one or number two; fix, close, or sell—were designed to bring focus and discipline to a company that had been complacent far too long.

He had one more such step in mind: cutting out excess layers of management.

All those layers slowed things down, Welch thought, and prevented senior managers from spotting trouble early enough. And ultimately, bureaucracy sapped the company's entrepreneurial spirit.

A FOUNDATION OF BUREAUCRACY

In the pre-Welch era, GE more or less assumed the existence of a large bureaucracy. In fact, "bureaucracy" was not a dirty word at GE. It implied a strong organization, a certain orderliness. There were bosses, and there were channels. People could "manage by memo," and that was assumed to be efficient.

But bureaucracy has a way of creeping. Of the company's 400,000 employees at the time of Welch's arrival, some 25,000 held the title of "manager." Approximately 500 were senior managers, and 130 were vice presidents or higher.

In other words, there was a huge officer corps, whose members did little except paperwork. They reviewed other people's memos and wrote memos to their own superiors.

One culprit was the planning system, which had grown cumbersome.

> We hired a head of planning and he hired two vice presidents and then he hired a planner, and then the books got thicker, and the printing got more sophisticated, and the covers got harder, and the drawings got better. The meetings kept getting larger. Nobody can say anything with 16 or 18 people there.

DELAYERING LETS PEOPLE FLOURISH

Welch decided to slice away at management in a process he called "delayering." He explicitly disagreed with critics who complained that getting rid of these levels would diminish GE's vaunted command-and-control capabilities and harm the company.

> We attempted to eliminate the command portion while keeping the subtleties of the control. Big corporations are filled with people in bureaucracy who want to cover things—cover the bases, say they did everything a little bit. Well, now

we have people out there all by themselves; there they are, accountable for their successes and their failures. But it gives them a chance to flourish. Now you see some wilt. That's the sad part of the job. Some who looked good in the big bureaucracy looked silly when you left them alone.

Welch had two goals in mind. First, he wanted to turn the strategic planning function over to the businesses. Second, he wanted to remove the obstacles that prevented direct contact among the businesses and between the business and the CEO's office. Control would survive; command would be diminished. The pace of business would pick up.

Delayering speeds communications. It returns control and accountability to the businesses, which is where it belongs.
We got two other great benefits from the sector delayering.
First, by taking out the biggest layer of top management, we set a role model for the whole company about becoming lean and agile.
Second, we identified the business leaders who didn't share the values we were talking about: candor, facing reality, lean and agile. We exposed the passive resisters.

In retrospect, Welch was convinced that he had acted properly by trimming GE's bureaucracy. "By the time you get through the levels, the barn has burned down, and you've got to get closer to the game," he said in 1997. "Every layer is a bad layer. Now we don't have all that nonsense. If Delhi wants something, they fax me."

Delayering requires a certain kind of resolve. It's one thing to lay off lower-level employees at distant factories, far from the corner offices. It's quite another to ax an associate, or a buddy, in the next office.

But this is the kind of resolve that may be needed to transform a low-performing organization into a higher-performing one or to push a high performer to the next level. Deadwood and redundancy in the executive suites can cost a company dearly in money, flexibility, and spirit.

WELCH RULES

➤ **Get rid of any layers of management that do not add real value to the process.** Ask yourself: How can I improve communications with the folks down below on the factory floor? If the answer is "lose layers," then lose them.

➤ **Don't let emotions get in the way.** Cutting executive jobs can be one of the most difficult decisions a manager has to make. Make the call based on objective criteria, not relationships.

LEADERSHIP SECRET 15

SPARK PRODUCTIVITY THROUGH THE "S" SECRETS: SPEED, SIMPLICITY, AND SELF-CONFIDENCE

FROM THE FILES OF JACK WELCH

It takes enormous self-confidence to be simple, particularly in large organizations. Bureaucracy is terrified by speed and hates simplicity.

In the late 1980s and early 1990s, Jack Welch began to outline a new vision for GE's future. In September 1989, for example, he noted:

> **The biggest mistake we could make right now is to think that simply doing more of what worked in the '80s will be enough to win the '90s. It won't. . . . We have to turn in the**

> **'90s to the software of our companies—to the culture that drives them.**

Welch summed up his prescription for that culture in three words: speed, simplicity, and self-confidence.

THE FIRST TWO "S'S": SPEED AND SIMPLICITY

Speed, obviously, meant having people make decisions in minutes. It meant cutting back on paper flow and staff work.

Simplicity, as Welch defined it, meant different things in different corners of the company:

> **To an engineer, it's clean, functional designs with fewer parts. For manufacturing, it means judging a process not by how sophisticated it is, but how understandable it is to those who must make it work. In marketing, it means clear messages and clean proposals to consumers and industrial customers.**
>
> **And most important, on an individual, interpersonal level, it takes the form of plain-speaking, directness—honesty.**

Writing to shareholders in 1995, Welch elaborated on the importance of simplicity:

> **Simple messages travel faster, simpler designs reach the market faster, and the elimination of clutter allows faster decision making.**

In the case of senior management, a critical component of simplicity is a powerful, easily graspable core message—a vision:

> **Whatever it is—we're going to be number one or number two, or fix/close/sell, or boundarylessness—every idea you present must be something you could get across easily at a cocktail party with strangers. If only afficionados of your industry can understand what you're saying, you've blown it.**

THE THIRD "S": SELF-CONFIDENCE

The third S, self-confidence, is intimately related to the first two. In fact, argues Welch, one can't really embrace simplicity without a healthy dose of self-confidence:

> **One of the hardest things for a manager is to reach a threshold of self-confidence where being simple is comfortable.**

Where does this self-confidence come from? Welch's answer has several parts:

> **Some people get it at their mother's knee, others through scholastic, athletic, or other achievement. Some tiptoe through life without it. If we are to create this boundaryless company, we have to create an atmosphere where self-confidence can grow in each of ... us.**

But many attributes of large organizations, such as the turf battles, the parochialism, and so on, work *against* the development of self-confidence:

> **Self-confidence does not grow in someone who is just another appendage on the bureaucracy, whose authority rests on little more than a title. Bureaucracy is terrified by speed and hates simplicity. It fosters defensiveness, intrigue, sometimes meanness.**

Even if a company can't manufacture self-confidence, says Welch, it can work against the confidence-destroying aspects of corporate culture. It can provide people with opportunities to dream, take risks, and win. And it can make sure that employees can see how their work contributes to the overall effort:

> **We can grow a work ethic that plays to our strengths, one that unleashes and liberates the awesome productive energy that we know resides in our work force. If we can ... create an environment where each man and woman who works in our companies can see a clear connection between what he or she does every day, all day, and winning and losing in the**

real world, we can become productive beyond our wildest dreams.

This was one reason GE devised its Work-Out program: to design a process that gave people a voice and got them talking to one another and learning to trust one another.

Again, the three S's are interrelated and mutually supportive. In his 1995 letter to shareholders, Welch commented:

> **Self-confident people don't need to wrap themselves in complexity, "businessese" speech, and all the clutter that passes for sophistication in business—especially big business.**
> **Self-confident leaders produce simple plans, speak simply, and propose big, clear targets.**

Speed. Simplicity. Self-confidence. They emerged and endured as key watchwords in the Welch management philosophy.

WELCH RULES

➤ Promote the three "S's": speed, simplicity, and self-confidence. These three attributes build organizations that are able to change with the changing environment.

➤ Start with a simple message. The most effective communications are those that are easy to understand. Making the vision clear sparks people's passion and productivity.

➤ Establish systems that foster self-confidence. Help people understand how their efforts are helping the company to succeed. Find ways to let people take risks and win.

LEADERSHIP
SECRET 16

ACT LIKE A SMALL COMPANY

Small companies move faster. They know the penalties for hesitation in the marketplace. What we are trying relentlessly to do is get that small-company soul—and small-company speed—inside our big-company body.

The goal of most big corporations is to get still bigger. Bigness is considered a virtue (or at least a necessary evil) in the corporate environment.

When Jack Welch took over at GE, the company was then one of the largest in America, with more than 400,000 employees. Through restructuring and downsizing, Welch pared the company down to 270,000 employees. But meanwhile, GE's acquisitions were adding many more people to the payroll, as was Welch's Six Sigma quality initiative. By the summer of 2000, GE had 340,000 employees.

But simple head counts can be misleading. Even as GE was

getting bigger, Welch was making his company *act* as if it were much smaller. He achieved this goal by simplifying GE's complex hierarchy and by creating programs that unleashed empowered workers.

BIG HAS ITS ADVANTAGES

Does "big" have its advantages? Of course, says Welch:

> Big allows us, for example, to spend billions on development of the new GE90 jet engine, or the next-generation gas turbine, or positron emission tomography [PET] diagnostic imaging machines—products that sometimes take years of investment before they begin producing returns.
>
> Size gives us staying power through market cycles in big, promising businesses ... Size will allow continued heavy investment in new products ... Size gives us the resources to invest over a half-billion dollars a year on education: cultivating, at every level in the organization, the human capital we must have to win.
>
> Offshore, "big" permits us to form partnerships with the best of the large companies, and large countries, and to invest for the long term in nations such as India, Mexico, and the emerging industrial powers of South Asia.

SMALL COMPANIES CUT TO THE CHASE

Big, it seems, can be beautiful. So what is it about small companies that Welch loves? His answer:

> For one, they communicate better.
>
> Without the din and prattle of bureaucracy, people listen as well as talk; and since there are fewer of them, they generally know and understand each other.
>
> Second, small companies move faster. They know the penalties for hesitation in the marketplace.
>
> Third, in small companies, with fewer layers and less cam-

ouflage, the leaders show up very clearly on the screen. Their
performance and its impact are clear to everyone.

And finally, small companies waste less. They spend less
time in endless reviews and approvals and politics and paper
drills. They have fewer people; therefore they only do the important things. Their people are free to direct their energy
and attention toward the marketplace rather than fighting
bureaucracy.

Welch loves the idea that small companies are uncluttered,
simple, and informal.

They thrive on passion and ridicule bureaucracy. Small
companies grow on good ideas—regardless of their source.

They need everyone, involve everyone, and reward or remove people based on their contribution to winning. Small
companies dream big dreams and set the bar high; incre-
ments and fractions don't interest them.

And he loves the way small companies communicate:

with simple, straightforward, passionate argument rather
than jargon-filled memos, "putting it in channels," "running it
up the flagpole," and worst of all, the polite deference to the
small ideas that too often come from big officers in big companies.

Everyone in a small company knows the customers—their
likes, dislikes, and needs—because the customers' thumbs-up
or [thumbs]-down means the difference between a small
company becoming a bigger company tomorrow or no company at all.

So size alone, says Welch, is no longer enough in a brutally
competitive world marketplace. Big companies must acquire the
soul of a small company. While you are growing, Welch cautions,
don't lose your soul.

Don't permit the attributes of bigness to overwhelm you.

Get bigger, but protect the soul of the more nimble organization that you once were.

WELCH RULES

➤ Assume that your big company can act small. Welch
had to work at it, but he knew he could instill the

passion and informality of a small company into the soul of GE.

➤ **Structure for smallness.** Welch removed layers and sector heads that did not add value. If your organization is too bloated, consider restructuring, removing layers, boundaries, approvals—in short, anything that bloats and slows the company.

➤ **Check reality: Do you know your customers?** This is a good yardstick. Welch likes to compare his company to the corner grocery store. Do you know your customers, and do they know you? If not, you have your work cut out for you.

LEADERSHIP SECRET 17

REMOVE THE BOUNDARIES!

Our people must be as comfortable in New Delhi and Seoul as they are in Louisville or Schenectady...

When Jack Welch came on board, General Electric had hundreds of boundaries.

Those boundaries kept people within the company from communicating easily with one another. And by extension, they kept GE personnel from communicating with outside constituents.

When Jack Welch assumed command, he tried to identify all the debilitating boundaries within GE. He knew that if he could eliminate boundaries, it would go far toward creating the open, informal business environment that he believed was essential.

THE GENESIS OF BOUNDARYLESS

Welch called upon GE to become *boundaryless*. The term was certainly not in any dictionary. And as Welch was quick to acknowledge, the made-up word was clumsy at best. But people soon understood what it meant.

Welch first began using the term in the early 1990s. At that time, he acknowledged that the business strategies he had employed in the 1980s—restructuring, reducing the number of management layers, and the like—were too incremental. They took too long to affect the company.

Something new was needed. The answer was *boundaryless*.

WHAT'S IN A WORD?

The boundaryless company, Welch notes, is one in which "we knock down the walls that separate us from each other on the inside, and from our key constituents on the outside." The boundaryless company:

- Removes barriers between functions
- Removes barriers between levels
- Removes barriers between locations
- Reaches out to important suppliers and makes them part of a single process

We no longer have the time to climb over barriers between functions like engineering and marketing, or between people—hourly, salaried, management, and the like.

How does one get rid of boundaries? At GE, it was easiest to get rid of the vertical ones—the boundaries of hierarchy—and the company made great strides in this area in the 1980s.

What happens after getting rid of the boundaries?

Instead of hierarchies, there are cross-functional teams.

Instead of managers, there are business leaders.

Instead of workers who are told what to do, there are workers who decide what to do.

> **If you want to get the benefit of everything employees have, you've got to free them—make everybody a participant. Everybody has to know everything, so they can make the right decision by themselves.**

By the summer of 1993, boundarylessness had become one of the core values at GE:

> **If you're turf-oriented, self-centered, don't share with people, and are not searching for ideas, you don't belong here . . .**
>
> **Being boundaryless allows us to jab one another and have fun. We rag each other when somebody starts to protect turf.**

THE CEC MODEL

One powerful force for boundarylessness at GE is the Corporate Executive Council (CEC), which includes the top 25 to 30 executives of the company. It meets every 3 months, from a Monday to a Wednesday, for a free-flowing exchange of ideas.

In the bad old days, says Welch, GE functioned like a classic conglomerate. "Each business quarter," he explains, "the divisional manager phoned the finance person to report the numbers."

GE is very different today. Through the CEC, leaders don't merely discuss numbers; they exchange ideas.

By design, CEC sessions have no formal agenda. The point is to *keep it loose.*

A senior GE official may distribute a brief memo in advance of the get-together to alert the executives about the main topic of the meeting. But that's about it in terms of structure. The whole purpose of the meeting is to foster learning about problems being faced by other businesses and to pick up good ideas that might work in one's own business. Structure would work against these goals.

The CEC is, in a sense, a model and metaphor. Welch urged his colleagues at GE to *break down boundaries*, wherever they existed, from the CEC level on down. The fewer the boundaries, the more likely that employees could do their jobs well.

WELCH RULES

➤ **Root out boundaries.** Anything that disrupts communications between departments and employees or between employees and outside constituents is bad.

➤ **Model behaviors with senior managers.** Welch credits his CEC meetings with helping to spread the flow of ideas throughout all of GE's diverse businesses. They also set a positive pattern for others in the company.

➤ **Involve everybody.** To achieve boundarylessness in your organization, involve everybody. If boundaries are deeply ingrained, consider holding a Work-Out session (see Leadership Secrets 18 to 20).

LEADERSHIP SECRET 18

UNLEASH THE ENERGY OF YOUR WORKERS

FROM THE FILES OF JACK WELCH

The way to get faster, more productive, and more competitive is to unleash the energy and intelligence and raw, ornery self-confidence of the American worker, who is still by far the most productive and innovative in the world.

The first phase of Jack Welch's revolution at GE, in the early 1980s, brought massive change:

- 350 businesses transformed into 12
- The core electrical manufacturing businesses replaced by high-tech and service as the focus of the company
- Selected plants closed, and others made state of the art
- Payrolls slashed, and layers of management pared away

Jack Welch called these years the "hardware phase." And although the hardware phase boosted GE's bottom line, it also disconcerted many employees. They had been moved to new plants, given new bosses, assigned new tasks. As a result, few felt secure in the new GE.

By the late 1980s, Welch knew that a serious issue confronted him. As a result of downsizing, GE's remaining employees were expected to carry a far greater work burden. They had to develop the belief that they were not just cogs in a giant machine but valued contributors.

They had to be made to feel like *owners*.

TURN EMPLOYEES INTO OWNERS

This was a tall order. At the time, a spirit of animosity prevailed between management and workers.

"We spent 90 percent of our time on the floor figuring out how to screw the management," an employee later confessed to Welch. "That was all right because you guys spent 95 percent of your time figuring out how to screw us."

So in the fall of 1988, Welch launched the second phase of his revolution. It centered on shifting authority from managers to employees.

> **The way to harness the power of these people is to protect them, not to sit on them, but to turn them loose, let them go—get the management layers off their backs, the bureaucratic shackles off their feet, and the function barriers out of their way.**

In the past, managers had carried the burden of boosting productivity; from now on, this would become the job of the men and women on the factory floor.

> **Before at GE, we generally used to tell people what to do. And they did exactly what they were told to do and not**

one other thing. Now we are constantly amazed by how much people will do when they are not told what to do by management.

A new concept had been born. Welch gave it a name: *empowerment*.

As GE managers were fond of saying, workers tended to park their brains at the factory gate each morning. No longer! Henceforth, managers had to find a way to harness the brainpower of the work force. They had to permit workers to make decisions, contribute ideas, and organize their own workdays. They had to give their employees more power, make their workday more fun and interesting, and otherwise enable them to raise their own level of productivity.

Welch later confessed that he regretted having waited 7 years to empower the work force. But starting earlier would have been impractical. In the "hardware phase," there was too much uncertainty, as employees worried whether they would still have a job at the end of each day. And of course, there were too many bureaucrats.

Empowering and liberating and exhilarating a bloated bureaucracy in the beginning would have been impossible. It would have produced a mixed message because we were shocking them. I'm not sure you could have sold that and been credible.

In 1990, Welch unleashed the next phase of his "empowerment revolution": a program he called Work-Out. As we will see shortly, Work-Out was all about building up employees and showing them that they were contributing directly to the health of the enterprise.

Welch had at least one ulterior motive in effecting all this change. He continued to be irritated by Wall Street's persistent assessment of GE as a portfolio of businesses lacking coherence and focus. A spirit of common purpose would eventually impress outsiders and perhaps even the skeptics on Wall Street.

But this was a secondary concern. At their heart, Welch's

changes were about treating employees as an integral part of the business.

WELCH RULES

➤ **Unleash productivity by involving everyone.** Make sure that everyone knows how important his or her contribution is to the overall effort.

➤ **Turn workers into owners.** Owners—literal and figurative—have a far greater stake in the business.

➤ **Have patience; attitudes don't change overnight.** Welch waited until 1988 before implementing Work-Out. He knew that other aspects of his plan had to take effect before he could make his move.

LEADERSHIP SECRET 19

LISTEN TO THE PEOPLE WHO ACTUALLY DO THE WORK

FROM THE FILES OF JACK WELCH

Our desire to tap into this creativity ... to listen more clearly to these ideas ... led us to a process we call Work-Out.

The subject of this chapter began as a GE paradox.

Jack Welch, one of the country's toughest and most aggressive bosses, brought forth a program designed to let workers become their own bosses.

By doing so, he changed his company.

THE NAME AND THE MODEL

Like all ambitious programs, this one needed a name.

Welch had been talking about "working out the nonsense of GE" and dealing with problems that needed to be "worked out." Not surprisingly, the name became "Work-Out."

The model for Work-Out was the New England town meeting in which residents charted the town's course through dialogue with each other and with the town leaders. Welch hoped the Work-Out program would help GE accomplish four important goals:

1. Develop trust among employees
2. Empower employees
3. Eliminate unnecessary work
4. Spread the GE culture

At the heart of Work-Out were two assumptions:

1. Employees had to be in a position to make suggestions to their bosses face-to-face.
2. Employees had to be able to get a reply on the spot, when possible.

Work-Out began in the fall of 1990. Welch wanted all GE employees to complete at least one Work-Out session within a year. Thus, the initial emphasis was on getting as many employees through the program as possible rather than on developing and refining specific techniques.

THE SPECIFICS

Once organizers decided who should attend a Work-Out session, they sent out invitations, explaining what Work-Out was all about. A subsequent letter, containing details about when and where the session would occur, was mailed to those who expressed interest.

The sessions were conducted far enough from the workplace, often at a hotel, to get people's undivided attention. Workshops usually lasted 3 days. There might be as many as 50 participants or as few as 20. They represented a cross section of GE personnel from senior and junior managers to salaried and hourly workers. During the first 2 days, no one was allowed to take notes. (Welch was concerned that taking notes would "bureaucratize" the exercise.)

Generally, the leader of any GE business, large or small, kicked off the first-day session, talking about the strengths and weaknesses of that business and explaining how the business fit into GE's overall strategy. Then, for the time being, he or she left.

A facilitator then arranged for participants to break up into small groups of 8 to 12 people. The groups brainstormed about some of the weaknesses the keynote speaker had identified. The facilitator shuttled from one room to another, keeping the breakout sessions on track.

The facilitator had no veto power over what topics were discussed. However, he or she was concerned with process. In particular, senior employees weren't allowed to dominate conversations or bully others in the room.

Eventually, the facilitator reconvened the minigroups in a plenary session. The participants then discussed their ideas about the business's problems, paying particular attention to four criteria: reports, meetings, measurements, and approvals. What should be eliminated? What should be reinforced? Their ideas were summarized in a series of proposals, which might number as many as two dozen or more.

In the final hours of the third day, the boss returned to undergo a fairly remarkable experience.

TURNING HIERARCHY UPSIDE DOWN

It was this final session that gave Work-Out its special power. For 2 full days, employees had spent hours discussing not only their business but also their boss. Employees were expected to be completely candid in their critiques of both, and most often, they were.

The result was a fairly dramatic shift of power. Previously, the boss, standing in the front of the room, had an unchallenged aura of authority. No more! Now, the boss had to listen and learn.

The participants put forward their proposals, and the boss could make one of three responses: (a) agree, (b) say no, or (c) seek more information. In this last case, the manager would be required to come up with an answer within a month.

The big surprise? Some *80 percent* of the proposals got immediate up-or-down answers. Work-Out suggested that, given the right circumstances, it's not difficult to reach decisions and make changes in a business.

A participant was chosen to record all the proposals discussed, along with the steps to be taken by management to determine the feasibility of a certain proposal. After all other participants certified the accuracy of this summary, it was distributed to everyone else in that particular GE business.

Next to each recommendation was the name of the Work-Out participant who raised the issue—the issue's "champion"—who followed up on the recommendation and informed the attendees of progress.

The goal of Work-Out was to come up with specific, actionable items. (Recommendations with fuzzy language were dropped.) Each recommendation could comprise as many as three action items, and each action item came with a deadline. The Work-Out leader assigned a "roadblock buster," who made sure that each deadline was met.

WELCH RULES

➤ **Turn hierarchy upside down.** The Work-Out program was clear evidence of Welch's commitment to transferring power within GE. Managers who could not deal with the requirements of Work-Out were fired.

➤ **Enable people to speak out freely.** The success of this sort of program depends on employees speaking candidly, without fear of penalty.

➤ **If a full-blown Work-Out session is not possible, consider a half-day minisession.** Follow the guidelines presented in this leadership secret but compress the entire session into a half-day program.

LEADERSHIP SECRET 20

GO BEFORE YOUR WORKERS AND ANSWER ALL THEIR QUESTIONS

FROM THE FILES OF JACK WELCH

The people who are closest to the work really do know it better.

At the outset of the Work-Out program, the invisible walls between managers and employees often loomed large and inhibited communication between the two constituencies.

The chains of history and tradition were too strong to be broken so quickly. Initially, there were many awkward silences.

But over time, Work-Out began to catch on. Someone would summon up the necessary courage and talk.

A question would get asked.

A problem would be put on the table.

Once the ice was broken, others in the audience overcame their timidity as well. And then things started to happen.

A CASE IN POINT

Armand Lauzon, a GE manager, faced Work-Out attendees (from a GE facility in Lynn, Massachusetts) on the final day of a session.

One by one, the group's 108 recommendations were put to him for one of three responses: "yes," "no," or "need more information." The proposals ranged from designing a plant-service insignia to building a new tinsmith shop.

To 100 of the 108 proposals, Lauzon said "yes" on the spot.

One of the approved proposals was to permit Lynn's employees to bid against an outside vendor on new protective shields for grinding machines. (An hourly worker had sketched a design for the shields on a brown paper bag.) Ultimately, the internal group won the bid for $16,000, far less than the vendor's quoted $96,000. It was an ideal Work-Out result: saving GE money, bringing work to the Lynn plant, and empowering employees.

RATTLERS AND PYTHONS

At some Work-Out sessions, facilitators divided problems into two separate categories: rattlers and pythons.

Rattlers were problems that could be resolved on the spot; that is, they could be shot and buried in real time, like a rattlesnake.

Pythons, by contrast, were issues that were too complicated to unravel straight away, comparable to a python wrapped up in itself.

One rattler example involved a young woman who published a popular monthly plant newspaper and had run into a wall of bureaucracy. GE policies required her to secure *seven signatures* before she could go to press. She pleaded her case to her boss at a Work-Out session: "You all like the plant newspaper. It's never been criticized. It's won awards. So why does it take seven signatures?"

"This is crazy," he replied. "Okay, from now on, no more signatures."

At the Research and Development Center in Schenectady, New York, an employee at a Work-Out session asked why managers got special parking places. No one could think of a good reason. The privilege was rescinded on the spot.

At a Work-Out session for the company's communications personnel, a secretary asked why she had to interrupt her own work each time something landed in the "out tray" on her boss's desk. Why couldn't he drop the material off on her desk the next time he left his office? On the spot, the change was made.

Pythons, by definition, are tougher to unwind than rattlers.

At one Work-Out session, field-service engineers griped about having to write reports used to forecast which turbines might need to be replaced the next time an outage occurred.

Their complaint was that no one was *reading* the reports, which sometimes ran as long as 500 pages.

This problem was knottier. People actually did need some version of this information, although clearly not in its current form.

Eventually, as a result of some intense Work-Out sessions, the huge reports were scrapped. In their place came briefer, more up-to-date reports, which were actually read!

THE KEY ELEMENT

Jack Welch, for one, was ecstatic about Work-Out:

> **Work-Out is many things ... but its central objective is "growing" a culture where everyone's ideas have value ... where leaders lead rather than control [and] coach rather than kibitz.**
> **Work-Out is the process of mining the creativity and productivity that we know resides in the American work force ...**

In 1997, Welch spoke again as an advocate of high employee involvement:

> **The most important thing a leader has to do is to absolutely search and treasure and nourish the voice and dignity of every person. It is in the end the key element.**

The Work-Out program continues today. According to one senior executive, it has proven itself as a "best practice which targets bureaucracy and all its waste, pomposity, and nonsense."

WELCH RULES

➤ Search out practices that have stopped making sense. Every company has these foolish habits that should have been abolished years ago. Root them out and eliminate them.

➤ Build programs on a foundation like Work-Out. Think of Work-Out as a prerequisite to more ambitious initiatives such as Six Sigma.

➤ Nourish dignity. The most important thing a leader does, Jack Welch asserts, is "treasure and nourish the voice and dignity of every person."

PART IV

NEXT-GENERATION LEADERSHIP: INITIATIVES
FOR DRIVING AND SUSTAINING
DOUBLE-DIGIT GROWTH

LEADERSHIP SECRET 21

STRETCH: EXCEED YOUR
GOALS AS OFTEN AS YOU CAN

FROM THE FLIES OF JACK WELCH

Boundaryless people, excited by speed and inspired by Stretch dreams, have an absolutely infinite capacity to improve everything.

Most managers feel that reaching goals and meeting budgets translate into doing a good job.

That's not good enough for Jack Welch.

He feels that goals exist to be exceeded and even to be blown away. He calls this business strategy "Stretch."

Set the bar very high, advises Welch. If you don't, you'll never know how much your workers can really achieve.

MAKING STRETCH HAPPEN

Stretch begins with the definition of performance targets that are within a company's capabilities.

The second aspect involves setting those sights higher—much higher—toward goals that seem beyond reach, requiring an almost superhuman effort to achieve.

> **We have found that by reaching for what appears to be the impossible, we often actually do the impossible; and even when we don't quite make it, we inevitably wind up doing much better than we would have done.**

Reaching and stretching, according to Welch, avoid the mediocrity that can arise out of compromise:

> **People work for a month on charts and presentations and books to come in and tell the CEO that, given the economic environment, given the competitive scenario, the best they can do is a 2. Then the CEO says, "I have to give the shareholders a 4." They eventually settle on 3 and everyone goes home happy.**

So Stretch means shooting for the stars. But what happens if employees fail to reach goals? Welch considers this a crucial Stretch issue.

> **If they don't have the team operating effectively, you give them another chance. If they fail again, you hand the reins to another person. But you don't punish for not meeting big targets.**
>
> **If 10 is the target and you're only at 2, we'll have a party when you go to 4. We'll give out bonuses and go out on the town and drink or whatever. When you reach 6, we'll celebrate again. We don't waste time and money budgeting 4.12 to 5.13 to 6.17.**

Jeff Immelt, former head of GE Medical Systems who ultimately succeeded Jack Welch as CEO, observed that when Welch began the Stretch concept in the early 1990s, he focused on financial goals. By the late 1990s, he was concentrating on getting

GE business leaders to stretch goals dealing with process (the new introduction of products, cycle time, etc.). "You'll never get there if you don't do process," says Immelt.

STRETCH DOES HAVE RISKS

Too much Stretch can be a bad thing.

"It makes you think that your plan won't get you to the Stretch goal," explains David Calhoun, head of GE Lighting in the late 1990s. "So you might think about acquiring a new company, [or you] might decide to drop prices out of the bottom to get to the Stretch goal. In other words, stretching forces them to do stuff they wouldn't otherwise do."

And Stretch can lead to internal frictions. There was the example of a lower level employee who worked hard to improve on the previous year's numbers. At the end of the year, that person did indeed get his numbers up. Yet the person's boss, who was seeking a far higher Stretch target, scolded the worker for "only delivering" what the boss deemed to be mediocre results.

The result, not surprisingly, was an unhappy manager and an unmotivated employee.

Welch understands that Stretch is not an easy concept, and it takes time to implement.

> **If you have a lousy relationship where a boss takes a Stretch goal and stamps it as a plan and then nails you because you didn't reach it, the Stretch program is dead.**

WORTH THE RISKS

To some business leaders, Stretch may be out of reach.

And indeed, in Welch's early years, Stretch was out of reach for GE. It would have been too much to ask of his GE colleagues in the difficult years of restructuring. They first needed to regain confidence in themselves and in their businesses. Once they did, Stretch became possible.

Reach for the stars, Welch exhorted his people.

The worst that can happen is that you will fail.

Indeed, you probably *will* fail.

But by stretching yourself and stretching your business, you may actually *reach* the stars.

WELCH RULES

➤ **Get the most out of your employees.** Each employee should be "stretched" to the maximum.

➤ **Set Stretch goals and then push to exceed them.** If people don't reach those goals, fine—as long as they've truly tried to stretch.

➤ **Push for the impossible.** Instill in your employees the idea that they should go beyond ordinary goals.

LEADERSHIP
SECRET 22

MAKE QUALITY A TOP
PRIORITY

FROM THE FILES OF JACK WELCH

*As boundaryless learning has defined how
we behave, Six Sigma quality will ... define
how we work.*

When Jack Welch embraces an idea, that idea becomes a
passion. This was true when he embraced quality—specifically, "Six Sigma" quality—in the late 1990s. He was convinced that focusing on quality would make General Electric the
most competitive company on earth.

A HIDDEN FACTORY

GE had long been associated with quality. But in the 1990s, it was becoming painfully clear that GE's quality was not world class.

> It's gotten better with each succeeding generation of product and service. But it has not improved enough to get us to the quality levels of that small circle of excellent global companies that had survived the intense competitive assault by themselves, achieving new levels of quality.

It wasn't as if Welch had ignored quality. But he had assumed that he could attack the issue of quality through other strategies. For example, the Work-Out program captured Welch's most important "cultural" goals: openness, informality, boundarylessness, high involvement, self-confidence, productivity, and so on. Welch hoped that Work-Out (among other efforts) would help keep GE's quality high.

But by the mid-1990s, employees were arguing that greater productivity was not possible without higher quality standards. Too much time was being spent on reworking products. One senior manager referred to the "hidden factory" in which all of that reworking went on.

So Welch gradually became convinced that being as good as the next guy, or even a little better, wasn't good enough.

> We want to be more than that. We want to change the competitive landscape by being not just better than our competitors but by taking quality to a whole new level. We want to make our quality so special, so valuable to our customers, so important to their success, that our products become their only real value choice.

The question was: *How?*

As it turned out, the answer was Six Sigma. Simply put, this measures mistakes per million operations. One sigma means that 68 percent of the products are acceptable. At six sigma, only 3.4 defects per million operations occur.

Pressure from Japanese competitors convinced American companies like Motorola that it was time to rethink things. The quality of American goods was then hovering at around four sigma levels. Japanese manufacturers of products like electric equipment, cars, and precision instruments were already at six sigma levels.

In the late 1980s and early 1990s, Motorola pioneered Six Sigma, increasing its quality from four sigma to five point five sigma. This yielded $2.2 billion in savings, and other companies soon launched their own Six Sigma programs.

A PHILOSOPHICAL PROBLEM

So Welch found himself in a dilemma.

He agreed that GE needed to push quality improvement. But he worried that Six Sigma was inconsistent with his business strategies. It was centrally managed. It seemed too bureaucratic with its reports and standard nomenclature. It assumed specific, agreed-upon measures.

Work-Out had been designed to *eliminate* reports, approvals, meetings, and measures. Six Sigma seemed likely to put them back in. "I don't know that it's us," he told one colleague.

THE CONSENSUS: WE NEED QUALITY

In April 1995, a survey showed that GE employees were dissatisfied with the quality of the company's products and processes. Many of them knew that a number of other companies had achieved dramatically higher quality levels through a disciplined, rigorous approach.

A few months later, Larry Bossidy reinforced the message. Bossidy had been a GE vice chairman, but he left in July 1991 to become CEO of AlliedSignal, where (in 1994) he launched a Six Sigma program.

"GE is a great company," Bossidy told GE's leaders. "I know. I worked there for 34 years. But there is a lot you can do to become greater. If GE decides to do it, you'll write the book on quality."

Welch was impressed. Ultimately, he and his colleagues decided that GE had to put together a serious quality program. But they also decided to do it in a way that was *special.*

As former Vice Chairman Paolo Fresco commented: "When GE decides to do something, it goes after its own objectives with a vengeance, with an intensity which is unique."

Within a few years, Six Sigma had become more than a GE program.

It had become the new corporate mantra—a *battle cry*, as much as a quality initiative.

WELCH RULES

➤ **Tackle quality head-on.** Don't rely on other company initiatives or strategies to tackle the problem of quality. Attack it directly.

➤ **Find the "hidden factory."** Don't let low quality standards necessitate endless reworking.

➤ **Use quality to make sure that your products are your customers' only actual value choice.** Quality can be just as important as price, features, and so on.

LEADERSHIP SECRET 23

MAKE QUALITY THE JOB OF EVERY EMPLOYEE

FROM THE FILES OF JACK WELCH

By 2000, we want to be not just better in quality, but a company 10,000 times better than its competitors.

In January 1996, at the annual gathering of GE's 500 top managers, Jack Welch formally launched the Six Sigma initiative. GE aimed to become a Six Sigma quality company by the year 2000, producing nearly defect-free products, services, and transactions.

Welch considered Six Sigma the most difficult Stretch goal GE had ever undertaken. But if successful, he said, the program would be "the biggest opportunity for growth, increased profitability, and individual employee satisfaction in the history of our company."

GOING FOR SIX SIGMA

Prior to Six Sigma, GE's typical processes generated about 35,000 defects per million operations, or three point five sigma. GE's goal through the Six Sigma program was to cut defects to fewer than four per million operations. To reach six sigma, therefore, GE needed to reduce its defect rates by 10,000 times. And to hit this goal by 2000, it would have to reduce defect levels an average of 84 percent a year. But Welch was optimistic:

> **Very little of this requires invention. We have taken a proven methodology, adapted it to a boundaryless culture, and are providing our teams every resource they will need to win. . . .**

Motorola had gotten to six sigma in 10 years. Welch wanted to get there in 5. Was this possible? Again, Welch was optimistic. Motorola had to pioneer the program. GE could learn from Motorola's experience and also had a Work-Out culture to reinforce the quality initiative.

> **There is no company in the world that has ever been better positioned to undertake an initiative as massive and transforming as this one. Every cultural change we've made over the past couple of decades positions us to take on this exciting and rewarding challenge.**

The Six Sigma program relied on the creation of a new "warrior class" within the company. This group—comprising Green Belts, Black Belts, and Master Black Belts—would be made up of managers who had undergone the complex statistical training of Six Sigma and could implement its procedures.

Despite Welch's enthusiasm, Six Sigma was at first considered by many to be another new management fad. So Welch turned up the heat. At the GE operating managers' meeting in January 1997, he hammered away at the importance of the quality program:

> **You've got to be lunatics about this subject. You've got to be passionate lunatics about the quality issue. You've got to be out on the fringe of demand, and pressure and push to make this happen. This has to be central to everything you do every day.**

Only the quality-minded individual, Welch warned, would prevail at GE:

> **In the next century, we expect the leadership of this company to have been Black Belt–trained people. They will just naturally only hire Black Belt–trained people. They will be the leaders who will insist only on seeing people like that in the company . . .**

Welch also put teeth behind his words. In March 1997, he sent a fax to GE managers around the world directly linking advancement opportunities to Six Sigma. Effective January 1, 1998, Welch wrote, one must have started Green Belt or Black Belt training to be promoted to a senior middle-management or senior management position. Effective January 1, 1999, all of GE's "professional" employees, numbering between 80,000 and 90,000, and including all officers, must have begun Green Belt or Black Belt training. And in case anyone still missed the point, Welch tied 40 percent of his 120 vice presidents' bonuses to progress toward quality results.

After Welch's fax, the number of applicants for Six Sigma training programs skyrocketed.

BACK TO THE LEARNING ORGANIZATION

A reporter asked Welch what the quality program meant to the average GE factory employee.

"Job security," Welch replied. "Enhanced satisfaction. Not wasteful rework. Growth." Without the quality program, he continued, the factory employee might get laid off. And because the quality program focused in part on *finding out what customers wanted*, the employee could increase his or her long-term job security.

This is a key point: Welch believes that quality is, at its heart, about the *customer*. When customers think they derive more value from *your* products and services, they remain your customers.

> **The drive for quality is not some GE drive. The only reason for the quality is to make your customers more competitive...**
>
> **It has nothing to do with what you want. All these things are done in a way that the customer drives them. The customer manages your factory.**

Welch insisted that the quality initiative was simply the next step in creating the learning organization:

> **Quality is the next act of productivity... Out of quality you eliminate reworking. You get salesmen's time improved dramatically. They're not spending 30 percent of their time on invoice errors....**
>
> **Quality is the next step in the learning process. Getting rid of layers. Getting rid of fat. Involving everyone. All that did was to get more ideas. The whole thing here is to create the learning organization.**

WELCH RULES

➤ Think about quality universally. When implementing a Six Sigmalike quality program, look at *all* products and processes.

➤ Start with a quality cadre. Welch identified a core group, with clear qualifications and characteristics, to lead the quality charge. Then he broadened the base.

➤ Link compensation to quality performance. As soon as pay and promotion prospects were linked to Six Sigma, participation soared and change took root.

LEADERSHIP SECRET 24

MAKE SURE EVERYONE UNDERSTANDS HOW SIX SIGMA WORKS

FROM THE FILES OF JACK WELCH

Quality is the next act of productivity.

Following Motorola's lead, General Electric designed a Six Sigma quality program comprising four steps to be applied to every process and transaction:

1. *Measure.* Identify the key internal process that influences "critical-to-quality" issues (CTQs) and measure the defects generated relative to identified CTQs. Defects are defined as out-of-tolerance CTQs. The end of this phase

comes when the Black Belt can successfully measure the defects generated for a key process affecting the CTQ.

2. *Analyze.* The objective of this phase is to learn why defects are generated. Brainstorming, statistical tools, and so on are used to spotlight key variables (Xs) that cause the defects. The output of this phase is the identification of the variables most likely to drive process variation.

3. *Improve.* The objective of this phase is to confirm the key variables and then: (a) quantify the effect of these variables on the CTQs, (b) identify the maximum acceptable ranges of the key variables, (c) make certain the measurement systems are capable of measuring the variation in the key variables, and (d) modify the process to stay within the acceptable ranges.

4. *Control.* The objective of this phase is to ensure that the modified process enables the key variables (Xs) to stay within the maximum acceptable ranges.

THE SIX SIGMA PLAYERS

There are four groups of key players in the GE Six Sigma effort:

1. *Champions.* These are senior managers who—although not on Six Sigma full time—define, approve, and fund projects and are responsible for the success of the overall program. Most Champions report directly to the business leader, and a GE business might have up to 10 Champions, each of whom receives a week's training. Several hundred Champions have been selected.

2. *Master Black Belts.* These are full-time teachers with heavy quantitative skills as well as teaching and leadership ability. They mentor Black Belts. Master Black Belts are trained for at least 2 weeks. In the fall of 2000, there were 500 Master Black Belts.

3. *Black Belts.* These are full-time quality executives who lead teams and report to the Champions. In the fall of 2000, there were 5000 Black Belts.

4. *Green Belts.* These are members of Black Belt project teams who do not work on the projects full time and have other jobs in the company. In the fall of 2000, there were 100,000 Green Belts.

THE SIX SIGMA PROCESS

Each of the four phases—measure, analyze, improve, control—takes 1 month. Each begins with 3 days of training, followed by 3 weeks of "doing" and 1 day of formal review by the Master Black Belts and Champions.

A "successful" project is one in which (a) defects are reduced 10 times if the process began at less than three sigma (66,000 defects per million operations) or (b) there is a 50 percent reduction in cases where the process started at greater than three sigma.

GE defined five corporate measures to help its businesses track progress in the Six Sigma program:

1. *Customer Satisfaction.* Each business conducts customer surveys, asking customers to grade GE and the best in a category on critical-to-quality issues on a one-to-five scale, where five is the best. A defect is defined as less than best in a category or, even if best in a category, a score of three or less.

2. *Cost of Poor Quality.* There are three components: appraisal (mostly inspection), internal costs (largely scrap and rework), and external costs (mainly warranties and concessions).

3. *Supplier Quality.* GE tracks defects where the defective part either (a) has one or more CTQs out of tolerance

and therefore must be returned or reworked or (b) is received outside the schedule.

4. *Internal Performance.* GE measures the defects generated by its processes. The measure is the sum of all defects in relation to the sum of all opportunities (CTQs) for defects.

5. *Design for Manufacturability.* GE measures the percentage of drawings reviewed for CTQs and the percentage of CTQs designed to Six Sigma. Most new products are now designed with CTQs identified. This is an important step because the design approach often drives the defect levels.

THE VERDICT

Since Six Sigma began in January 1996, the results have far exceeded Welch's expectations. He noted the progress in his letter to shareholders:

> The Six Sigma initiative is in its fifth year—its fifth trip through the operating system. From a standing start in 1996, with no financial benefit to the company, it has flourished to the point where it produced more than $2 billion in benefits in 1999, with much more to come.

Consistently throughout this ramp-up period, Welch stressed that quality-mindedness was critical to success at, and by, GE:

> In the next century, we will neither accept nor keep anyone without a quality mindset, a quality focus. It has been remarked that we are just a bit "unbalanced" on the subject. That's a fair comment. We are.

WELCH RULES

➤ Understand the component parts of Six Sigma quality. Measure, analyze, improve, and control to achieve a new discipline in your company.

➤ **Nothing is more important than follow-through.** You will need to make sure that quality does not fall off in the future.

➤ **Your customers know quality.** Consider initiating customer surveys to assess your quality effort.

LEADERSHIP SECRET 25

MAKE SURE THE CUSTOMER FEELS QUALITY

FROM THE FILES OF JACK WELCH

It's really gone from a quality program to a productivity program to a customer satisfaction program to changing the fundamental DNA of the company.

In his 1999 letter to shareholders, Jack Welch proudly explained the program's impact on the company.

During the initial 2 years, he noted, GE had invested some $500 million in training its work force. It had also dedicated some of its best talent, literally thousands of employees, full time to Six Sigma projects.

Nearly every professional worker at GE had become a Green Belt, with 3 weeks of training and one Six Sigma project under his or her belt.

Another 5000 full-time Black Belts and Master Black Belts were starting and supervising Six Sigma projects. A number of those Master Black Belts and Black Belts had already been promoted into key leadership posts.

As for the financial returns from Six Sigma, they were better than expected. Savings in 1998 due to Six Sigma projects amounted to $750 million, over and above GE's investment. Billions more would be saved due to increased volume and market share.

In 1998, GE introduced its first major products designed for Six Sigma. These products were "designed" by customers and incorporated every feature the customer deemed critical to quality. The first such product was LightSpeed, a CT scanner that revolutionized medical diagnostics. Thanks to LightSpeed, a chest scan that once took 3 minutes to perform now took only 17 seconds.

SIX SIGMA AT WORK

Here are some other examples of how Six Sigma has worked at GE:

Example 1

GE's lighting business had a billing system that didn't mesh very well electronically with the purchasing system of Wal-Mart, one of GE's most important customers. This caused disruptions, delays in payments, and wasted time for Wal-Mart.

A GE Black Belt team secured a $30,000 budget and went to work. Within 4 months, defects dropped by 98 percent.

Example 2

Employees at GE's Capital Mortgage Corporation were handling 300,000 telephone calls a year from customers. When necessary, they relied on voice mail. Although GE personnel always returned these calls, sometimes it was too late: Customers had already taken their business elsewhere.

A team led by a Master Black Belt got involved. It discovered that one of the corporation's 42 branches was able to answer its phone calls the first time around. The team figured out how and spread the word across the other 41 branches, leading to millions of dollars of additional business.

CUSTOMERS FEEL VARIANCE

However, by 1999, Welch and his senior colleagues were aware of a major problem. Although the company was saving significant sums through Six Sigma, *customers weren't sensing these improvements.* Why? The answer lies in a concept called *variance.*

Consider a hypothetical example, presented in the chart on page 113.

It appears there have been substantial improvements in customer service: The mean delivery time has been cut from 17 to 12 days. But there are wide variances in the delivery times. Yes, customers sometimes received the product in 4 days but other times didn't receive it for 20 days. And although the average performance has been improved, lots of deliveries still take up to 20 days.

Welch focused on these still-frustrated customers:

> **These customers hear the sounds of celebration coming from within GE walls and ask, "What's the big event? What did we miss?" The customer only feels the variance that we have not yet removed.**

The challenge he laid out to his top managers was to turn the company's outlook "outside in." This meant two things: (a) measuring the parameters of customer needs and processes and (b) working toward zero variability.

He explained this new priority in the 1999 annual report:

Customer Dashboard: Customer XYZ
Dashboard Dial: Order to Delivery Time
Order by Order Delivery Times

Starting Point	After Project	
28 Days	29 Days	
Mean Aspect		
18	6	Big Change
6	10	
23	13	
5	4	
8	10	
16	13	
Variance Aspect		
19	10	No Change
33	20	
11	13	
Average Performance		
17 Days	12 Days	

Today, Six Sigma is focused squarely where it must be—on helping our customers win. . . . The objective is not to deliver flawless products and services that we think the customer wants when we promise them—but rather, what customers really want when they want them.

And a year later, he presented another Six Sigma status report to GE shareholders, this time against the backdrop of e-business:

We have the hard part, hundreds of factories and ware-houses, world-leading products and technology. We have a century-old brand identity and a reputation known and ad-

mired around the globe, all attributes that new e-business entrants are desperate to get. And we have one other enormous advantage—Six Sigma quality—the greatest fulfillment engine ever devised.

WELCH RULES

➤ Customers must be brought into the process. Make sure that your customers feel the results of your quality program as quickly as possible.

➤ Don't assume that the customer is as happy as you are. Monitor customer reaction to the initiative on a continuing basis.

➤ Keep the customer as the main focus. Make sure your employees are aware that the point is to satisfy customers.

LEADERSHIP SECRET 26

GROW YOUR SERVICE BUSINESS: IT'S THE WAVE OF THE FUTURE

FROM THE FILES OF JACK WELCH

The market is bigger than we ever dreamt.

In 1980, the year before Welch took over, GE was almost entirely a manufacturing enterprise, with 85 percent of revenues coming from manufacturing and only 15 percent from services.

The company had always been involved in services, but the service sector was regarded as something of an afterthought—known, tellingly, as the "aftermarket."

At first, GE saw the service sector as merely a source of some incremental business. But in time, company executives understood that a systematic focus on services could enlarge the potential markets of GE businesses many times over.

HIGHER RATES OF GROWTH FROM SERVICES

To Jack Welch and other GE executives, the point was not to give up on manufacturing. But it was clear that the service sector had the potential for much higher rates of growth. And service had another huge advantage: Profit margins were typically 50 percent higher on services than on manufactured products.

So a push began in the late 1980s to grow services. In 1990, GE derived 45 percent of its revenues from its service businesses—up substantially from the 1980 figure. Only 5 years later, in 1995, GE's nonmanufacturing business (financial services, aftermarket services, and broadcasting) had grown to just under 60 percent of total revenues.

In 1995, Welch pushed the service initiative to full throttle. And by the year 2000, manufacturing made up only 25 percent of the entire GE mix, while nonmanufacturing businesses made up the rest, for total nonmanufacturing revenues of just under $100 billion.

The most important engine in this service growth—indeed, the key engine of growth for all of GE—has been GE Capital Services (GECS). In 1999, GECS revenue reached $55.7 billion, or about half of GE's total revenue of $111.6 billion.

But also extremely helpful to GE's efforts in the service field was a hidden asset: its installed base of industrial equipment, including 9000 commercial jet engines, 10,000 turbines, 13,000 locomotives, and 84,000 major pieces of medical diagnostic equipment.

By October 1996, GE was bringing in $7.8 billion—fully 11 percent of its total revenues—through servicing that installed base. At the end of 1998, its product-service revenue exceeded $12 billion a year.

MAKE SERVICE A PRIMARY MARKET

In 1997, Welch was asked how far he was prepared to go toward becoming service oriented. Was he prepared to abandon certain production lines?

In response, Welch noted that customer demand was pulling the company in the direction of services, but there was clearly a point of diminishing returns:

> **We offer them complete solutions not so much in order to increase our equipment sales, but because they have a need for them. That said, we will always be a company that sells high-tech products. Without products, you're dead. You go out of business and become obsolete. If I fail to introduce a new medical scanner, how many hospitals are likely to come and see me for new services?**

It's worth noting that General Electric's increased emphasis on services can run counter to one of Welch's earlier business strategies: that all GE businesses must be either number one or two in their markets.

What's the challenge? A company that manufactures, say, widgets can define its market quite narrowly and thereby seize the number one or number two spot with relative ease. But when that same company begins to provide services, its market share may plummet because it may put itself into a new peer group of service-oriented firms.

Welch, for one, can live with these kinds of complications.

> **All these things you learn. If Jack Welch knew 17 years ago what he knows today, it would be a better company. This is a learning organization. I learn every day. Keep searching. I don't know diddly. I got guys here trying to learn more.**

WELCH RULES

➤ Think hard about the services that might be directly associated with your products. Is your company leaving money on the table by not pursuing aftermarket service opportunities?

➤ **Think equally hard about services that are further removed from your core product lines.** GE Capital Services—far from the light-bulb trade!—has been an astounding success.

➤ **Stay flexible.** As you make the move into services, be aware that some of your long-standing ideas about your business may need to be adjusted.

LEADERSHIP SECRET 27

TAKE ADVANTAGE OF
E-BUSINESS OPPORTUNITIES

FROM THE FILES OF JACK WELCH

While we are already generating billions in Web-based revenues, the contribution of e-business to GE has been so much more. It is changing this company to its core.

Jack Welch viewed tackling the Internet as the fourth major initiative of his tenure at the helm of GE, after Work-Out, globalization, and Six Sigma quality.

During the 1980s, GE went through a substantial modernization effort, in part to take advantage of emerging technologies. Exploiting the Internet was a natural extension of these efforts.

But large, established companies like GE needed time to figure out the Internet. Many of these companies, especially retailers, moved slowly onto the Internet, fearful of cannibalizing their long-established brick-and-mortar businesses. Many were unwilling or unable to trade away profits for speculative ventures into e-business. Yes, Wall Street loved the dotcoms in their heyday, but Wall Street also expected companies like GE to make money.

THE WAITING GAME

GE's relationship with the Internet dates back to October 1994, when GE Plastics set up the company's first Web site. This was a straightforward "brochureware" site that presented information aimed at its key audience of design engineers.

Three years later, GE Polymerland, the distribution arm of GE Plastics, became the first GE Web site to engage in electronic transactions. This was only a small step forward, however, because GE Plastics was still doing transactions both off-line and on-line.

So GE was neither an early mover on the Web nor a particularly adventurous player when it did move. To some extent, this reflects the Old Economy background of its CEO.

Welch earned his doctorate in chemical engineering at the University of Illinois in 1960. As the Internet gained increasing attention in the early and mid-1990s, Welch began to feel his way. He watched intently as other companies reacted to this new phenomenon.

Like many other executives, he was bemused by Wall Street's embrace of the dotcoms. And no doubt, he envied these start-ups' high valuations, but not so much that he was tempted to plunge his company into the Internet world at an early, untested stage.

So he watched and waited.

LATE, BUT NOT TOO LATE

For Welch, the year 1998 was a turning point. By that time, it seemed that everyone around him was using the Internet for one thing or another. His wife was making their vacation plans on the Web. His colleagues at corporate headquarters were shopping on-line. By Christmas 1998, Welch was persuaded that the Internet Revolution was here to stay.

At that point, most of GE's Web sites were like GE Plastics': essentially on-line brochures. "The epiphany," observed Pam Wickham, Manager, E-Business Communications and www.ge.com, "which Jack got toward the end of 1998, was the transaction piece, that this was the business model to pursue, that the Internet could provide a revenue stream."

So Welch issued a challenge: As quickly as possible, all GE businesses would build Web sites that were fully equipped to handle transactions.

When Welch issued his challenge, GE Polymerland's Web site generated revenues of only $10,000 a week. By the end of 1999, that figure had risen to $6 million a week, and by June 2000, the site was bringing in $15 million a week.

And of course, GE Polymerland was only one example among many. In response to Welch's challenge, GE's many businesses developed "e-businesses." Critical aspects of these businesses, such as sales, product development, and customer collaboration, began to be performed partially or totally on-line.

One of the most appealing benefits of an e-business is increased efficiency. Under the old system, for example, a number of people took part in the ordering and fulfillment processes. At each one of these "touch points," human error could enter the system. Such errors are all but eliminated on the Internet, where the customer gets the chance to "create" the kind of product he or she wants without intermediation.

Today, only a few years after Jack Welch's strong push toward the Internet, General Electric is widely regarded as one of the best examples of an Old Economy giant successfully embracing e-commerce.

WELCH RULES

➤ **Look before you leap into e-business.** Welch was criticized for being a late mover on the Internet, but GE avoided many of the problems on the "bleeding edge" of technology.

➤ **Look for appropriate e-business opportunities.** Web brochures are not enough. What products can you sell in cyberspace?

➤ **Take advantage of the Web's efficiencies.** E-business, with its minimal transaction costs, can be highly profitable. Elimination of human error in the order-fulfillment process can further enhance profitability.

LEADERSHIP
SECRET 28

MAKE EXISTING BUSINESSES INTERNET READY: DON'T ASSUME THAT NEW BUSINESS MODELS ARE THE ANSWER

FROM THE FILES OF JACK WELCH

E-business . . . is already so big and transformational that it has almost outgrown the bounds of the word "initiative."

Jack Welch acknowledges that GE may have been intimidated by the Internet in its early days:

> **Why wasn't the e-revolution launched by big, highly re-sourced, high-technology companies, rather than the small start-ups that led it? The answer may lie, as perhaps is true in GE's case, in the mystery associated with the Internet—the**

perception that creating and operating Web sites was Nobel Prize work—the realm of the young and wild-eyed.

THE MISCONCEPTION

But even after deciding in 1999 to move aggressively into e-business, Welch and his fellow GE executives labored under a misconception.

They had devised an Internet strategy anchored in the belief that there were Internet-savvy companies gunning for GE and its traditional business models. The GE executives lumped these presumed rivals together under a catch phrase: destroyyour-business.com.

Welch believed that GE itself would have to play the role of "GE killer"—that is, devising the new Internet-based business models that would supplant the old ones.

To prepare for these efforts, GE put together e-business teams consisting of young Internet-savvy types. Stationed in off-site locations, they were tasked with figuring out tomorrow's Internet business models. Once those models were identified, GE would pounce on them and adopt them before anyone else had the chance to do so.

But in May 1999, the teams of young Internet hotshots delivered a surprising report: There were no competitive threats out there to any of GE's businesses. GE was so far ahead of the pack, they said, that it really didn't need to worry about threats from new business models.

Nevertheless, argued the young people, GE had to make its traditional businesses Web-enabled. This would prevent customers from jumping ship to competitors.

CHANGE TO THE CORE

The young people were talking Welch's language. This wasn't brain surgery, as he liked to say. And so, in the spring of 1999, e-business leadership teams were formed in all GE businesses. Their mandate was to take GE's business models, modify them, get them Web enabled, and move business processes from off-line to on-line.

NBC was the attraction that lured Jack Welch to the Internet party. It was the first business in the GE stable to become deeply involved in the Internet.

> **Think about MSNBC. Think about cable. Now think about what you can do as you get into the Internet ... we can drive traffic to sites. We're communicating with millions of people every day in that business. How many offshoots can we develop? How many new things? I think CNBC.com will be an incredible property.**

These kinds of visions persuaded Welch to set his ambitious goal for GE's managers: Create and implement an Internet strategy before the end of 1999.

As he noted in the 1999 annual report:

> **E-business ... is already so big and transformational that it has almost outgrown the bounds of the word "initiative." While we are already generating billions in Web-based revenues, the contribution of e-business to GE has been so much more. It is changing this company to its core.**

Because 85 percent of its transactions were with other businesses, GE was well positioned to take advantage of the business-to-business (B2B) marketplace on the Internet. On the other hand, this was still largely uncharted territory.

"It's not as if you look at us versus our traditional competitors and say we've been resisting it while all these other guys have been doing it," said Gary Reiner, senior vice president and GE's chief information officer. "Business-to-business commerce over the Internet as we would define it today, in the kinds of businesses where we've been playing—we haven't been doing much of it, nor has anybody else."

Ultimately, Welch's Internet vision boiled down to three imperatives:

1. Keep upgrading people and retaining Internet-skilled talent.

2. Figure out how to leverage information technology to create a competitive advantage for your businesses that customers can see and feel.

3. Leverage information technology to support internal business processes.

WELCH RULES

➤ **Adapt your business model to the Internet.** Don't worry that your business model will not work on the Internet.

➤ **Think "Web enabled" rather than "Web threatened."** Your goal should be to take existing products and processes on-line rather than attempting to build up from zero.

➤ **Think inside and outside.** On the Internet, as in most aspects of business, the two key challenges are (a) to develop great people inside and (b) to present a compelling value proposition to the customer.

LEADERSHIP
SECRET 29

USE E-BUSINESS TO PUT THE FINAL NAIL IN BUREAUCRACY

FROM THE FILES OF JACK WELCH

There's no question. Channels will be different. Commerce will be different. People will communicate differently.

Convinced that yet another business revolution was underway, Jack Welch moved aggressively toward the Internet in 1999.

Welch wanted *every senior executive* at GE to share his passion for this new form of commerce, and he took steps to make that happen. He instructed each of GE's 12 businesses to select an e-commerce leader. He told the teaching staff at Crotonville to make sure that *every class* taught at the Leadership Institute in the coming year focused intensively on some aspect of e-business.

Welch also encouraged younger GE staffers to serve as Internet "mentors" to senior GE executives. These mentors were asked to work with their older colleagues for 3 to 4 hours a week, surfing the Web and evaluating competitors' sites. In short, the older executives were learning to organize their computers, and their minds, for work on the Internet.

Welch had his own mentor. He admitted that he was at best a C or C-minus student: "I'm not the fastest gun in town." But, he said, the process worked:

> It was this mentor-mentee interaction . . . that helped overcome the only real hurdle some of us had: fear of the unknown. Having overcome that fear, and experiencing the transformational effects of e-business, we find that digitizing a company and developing e-business models are a lot easier—not harder—than we had ever imagined.

BREAKING THE GLASS

There was much more to be done.

By June 1999, the e-business initiative had affected the 1000 or so individuals who made up the e-business teams as well as some 500 senior executives at GE.

But what about the other 340,000 GE employees, to whom Welch wanted to convey his excitement about the Internet, preferably in "Internet time"? By June 1999, fully 70 percent of GE employees were using e-mail, and there seemed no reason not to take advantage of that medium to reach employees instantaneously. Welch decided to use the Internet to brief employees on each quarterly senior management meeting.

In his first "e-brief," issued on June 7, 1999, Welch observed:

> We must have a "break-the-glass" mentality to get on top of this fast-moving subject. You will see fanatical commitment from the Business CEOs and from me on this subject.

The response to this first e-brief was remarkable. Energized by the opportunity to communicate with Welch directly for the first time, *6000 employees* fired off e-mails to the boss within 2 days.

Of course, Welch couldn't respond to each and every message in this mountain, and as the novelty wore off, the flow subsided. But something fundamental had changed. Formerly, Welch's direct contacts often were limited to his two dozen or so direct reports. But after the implementation of e-mail, he regularly received between 40 and 50 e-mails a day from all corners of the GE empire.

And of course, people were e-mailing each other across the company.

And they were e-mailing customers, suppliers, and everyone else in the GE extended network. Welch loved it:

> **It puts a small-company soul into that big-company body and gives it the transparency, excitement, and buzz of a start-up.**
>
> **It is truly the elixir for GE and others who relish excitement and change. E-business is the final nail in the coffin for bureaucracy at GE. The utter transparency it brings about is a perfect fit for our boundaryless culture and means everyone in the organization has total access to everything worth knowing.**

PART OF A BIGGER PICTURE

The first effect of GE's Internet effort, Welch said, was to further energize and refresh the company's previous initiatives:

> **For 20 years, we've been driving to get the soul of a small company into this sometimes muscle-bound, big-company body. We described the contribution of Work-Out, and there was more. We delayered in the '80s, eliminating many of the filters and gatekeepers. We got faster by reducing corporate**

> staff. . . . And we ridiculed and removed bureaucrats until
> they became as rare around GE as whooping cranes.
>   Every year we got better, faster, hungrier, and more
> customer-focused—until the day this elixir, this tonic, this
> e-business came along and changed the DNA of GE forever
> by energizing and revitalizing every corner of this company.

The Internet enabled GE to use the huge databases it had
compiled on customer processes in ways that directly benefited
those customers. In the future, said Welch, these benefits would
only increase:

> What we are rapidly moving toward is the day when "Dr.
> Jones," in Radiology, can go to her home page in the morn-
> ing and find a comparison of the number, and clarity, of
> scans her CT machines performed in the last day, or week, to
> more than 10,000 other machines across the world. She will
> then be able to click and order software solutions that will
> bring her performance up to world-class levels. And the per-
> formance of her machines might have been improved, on-
> line, the previous night, by a GE engineer in Milwaukee, To-
> kyo, Paris, or Bangalore.

Welch looked forward to the day when the chief engineer at
a local utility could check the heat rate and fuel burn of his
turbines—before he had coffee in the morning—to learn how
he stacked up against 100 other utilities.

And with a few mouse clicks, that same engineer could review
all the services that GE could provide to increase his facility's
competitiveness.

With the advent of the Internet, Welch noted, amazing new
things became possible.

WELCH ON THE NET

GE, argued Welch, was well positioned to exploit the Internet.
It already possessed the nuts-and-bolts skills and strengths that
other companies sorely lacked:

> **We already have that! We already have the hard stuff—
> over 100 years of a well-recognized brand, leading edge
> technology in both product and financial services, and a Six
> Sigma–based fulfillment capability. The opportunities
> e-business creates for large companies like GE are unlimited.**

In particular, it was the *speed* of e-business that got Welch's
adrenaline flowing:

> **The speed that is the essence of "e" has accelerated the
> metabolism of the company, with people laughing out loud
> at presentations of business plans for "the third quarter of
> next year" and other tortoiselike projections of action. Time
> in GE today is measured in days and weeks.**

And yet, Welch told shareholders in April 2000, some things
were constant:

> **You have undoubtedly read about the ongoing debate
> about New Economy companies versus Old Economy compa-
> nies and the advantages, or penalties, for being one or the
> other.**
> **The fact is the Old Economy/New Economy scenarios are
> just trendy buzzwords. There is now and will be in the future
> only one global economy. Commerce hasn't changed. There
> is, however, a new Internet technology that is fundamentally
> changing how business operates.**

One area in which Internet technologies were having a pro-
found impact, Welch noted, was the *measurement* of progress.
Like most traditional companies, GE had measured things like
revenues, net income, cashflow, and so on. In the Internet world,
of course, these would continue to be measured, but they would
now be measured far more frequently. In addition, new things
would be measured, and these measures would be grouped into
four "buckets": buy, make, sell, and strategic:

> **On our "buy" side, we now measure the number of auc-
> tions on-line, the percentage of the total buy on-line, and the
> dollars saved.**
> **On the "make" portion, the Internet is all about getting in-
> formation from its source to the user without intermediaries.**

The new measurement is how fast information gets from its origin to users and how much unproductive data gathering, expediting, tracking orders, and the like can be eliminated.

This tedious work in a typical big company is the last bastion—the Alamo—of functionalism and bureaucracy. Taking it out improves both productivity and employee morale.

On the "sell" side, the new measurements are number of visitors, sales on-line, percentage of sales on-line, new customers, share, span, and the like.

Welch noted that if GE got the components right (e.g., number of on-line visitors, percentage of sales on-line, etc.), traditional sales and net and cashflow measurements would follow.

In the end, all of this going on at GE is about using this transformational new technology to better serve customers and to be so good and so fast we become the global supplier of choice.

WELCH RULES

➤ Manage in Internet time, using the latest technologies. The Internet, in combination with intranets, allows managers to communicate instantly with employees.

➤ Reinvent the company to compete in Internet time. Think in terms of days and weeks rather than years. Exploiting Internet time will change the fundamentals of your business.

➤ Build on strengths. Success on the Internet in part grows out of being a fundamentally strong company.

AFTERWORD

In September 2001, Jack Welch retired as chairman and CEO of General Electric. He had been at the job for 20 years and 5 months. His memoirs, *Jack: Straight from the Gut,* were published that month, and while Welch acknowledged to me that he enjoyed the book signings more than writing the book, he could certainly feel satisfied at the book's warm reception. It remained on bestseller lists for 6 months. Welch was circumspect about the kinds of business activities he was pursuing in retirement. He engaged in business consulting, but his clients were kept confidential.

As was befitting the man who many called the greatest CEO of the era, Welch left General Electric in spectacularly better shape than when he took over in April 1981. For the year 2001, during which Welch served as chairman and CEO for the first 8 months, GE had revenues of $125.9 billion (down 3 percent) and earnings of $14.1 billion (up 11 percent). Due to an economic downturn and the September 11 terror attacks, GE came under enormous pressure. The stock dropped 16 percent.

But no one blamed Welch or, for that matter, his successor, Jeff Immelt. *Fortune* magazine named GE the "Most Admired Company" for the fifth year in a row and the *Financial Times* picked GE as the "World's Most Respected Company" for the fourth time.

The programs that Welch set in motion became part of his legacy. At the forefront were Six Sigma and digitization. As for Six Sigma, there were more than 6000 projects in 2001. With respect to e-business, GE generated $19 billion of incremental cost savings. His service initiative had grown to a $19 billion portion of GE's 2001 revenues.

But Welch's legacy would not be measured only in the numbers. He would be unhappy if it had been. To him, the "soft stuff"—the company's values—were uppermost. For instilling values that did so much for GE and for leading the way so remarkably, the company renamed the Crotonville (N.Y.) management institute the John F. Welch Learning Center. One could imagine a huge smile breaking out on the former chairman's face upon hearing that news.